Arranged by Dan Coates

CONTENTS

TITLE	PAGE
THE CHRISTMAS WALTZ	2
FROSTY THE SNOWMAN	5
HAVE YOURSELF A MERRY LITTLE CHRISTMAS	10
I'LL BE HOME FOR CHRISTMAS	13
IT'S THE MOST WONDERFUL TIME OF THE YEAR	16
JINGLE BELL ROCK	29
LET IT SNOW! LET IT SNOW! LET IT SNOW!	8
SANTA CLAUS IS COMIN' TO TOWN	20
SLEIGH RIDE	22
WINTER WONDERLAND	26

Cover Photograph: Christmas Candles & Baubles
© istockphoto.com/Liliboas

Copyright © MMIX by Alfred Music Publishing Co., Inc.
All Rights Reserved   Printed in USA

ISBN-10: 0-7390-6169-0
ISBN-13: 978-0-7390-6169-5

THE CHRISTMAS WALTZ

Words by Sammy Cahn
Music by Jule Styne
Arranged by Dan Coates

© 1954 SANDS MUSIC CORP.
Copyright Renewed and Assigned to CAHN MUSIC COMPANY and JULE STYNE.
JULE STYNE'S interest Controlled by PRODUCERS MUSIC PUBL. CO., INC. and Administered by CHAPPELL & CO., INC.
All Rights Reserved

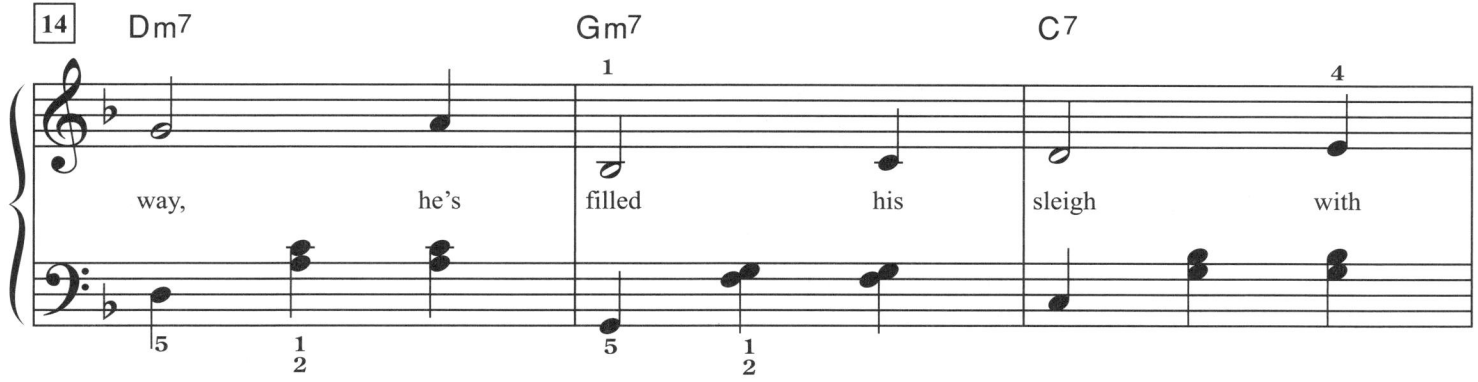
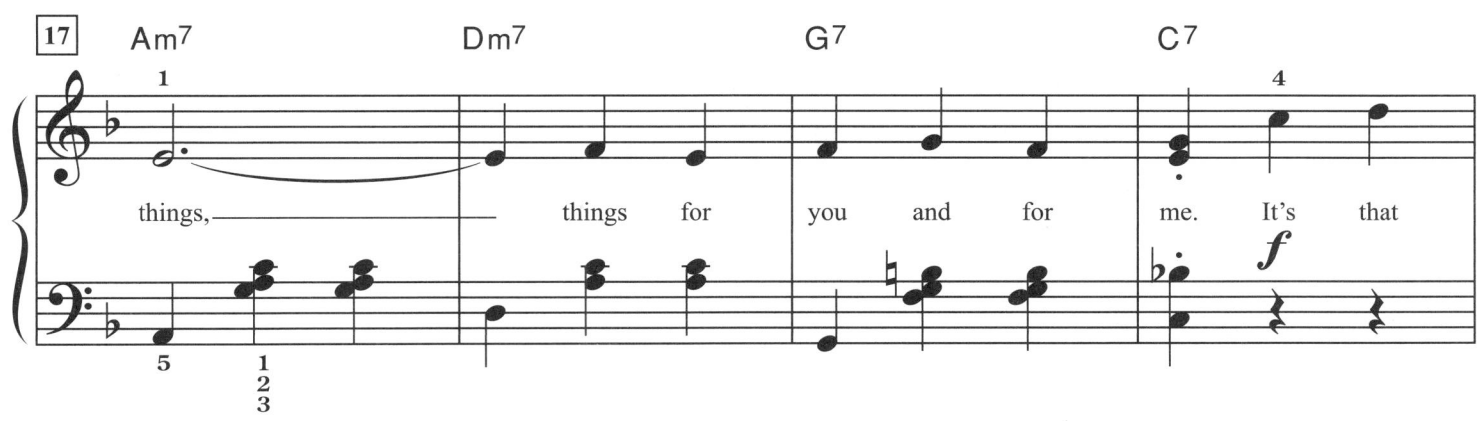
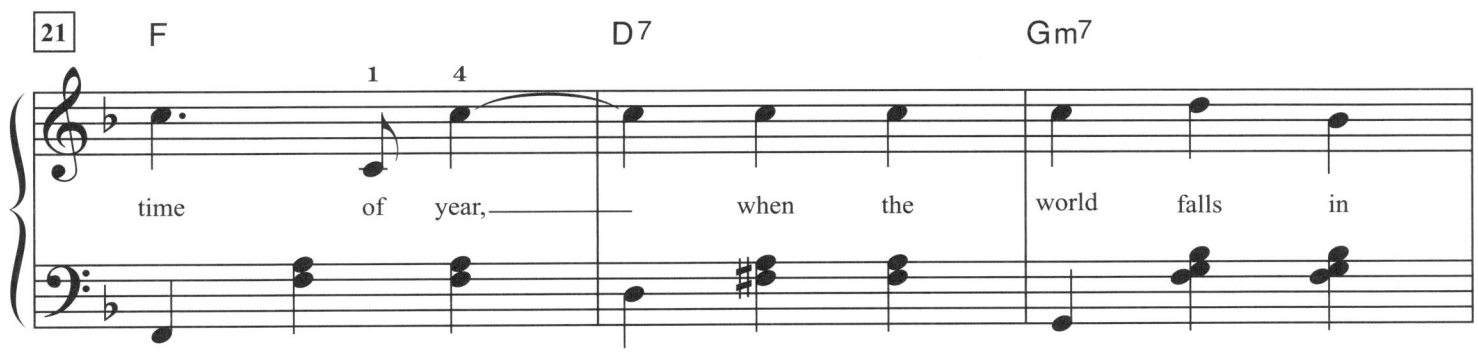

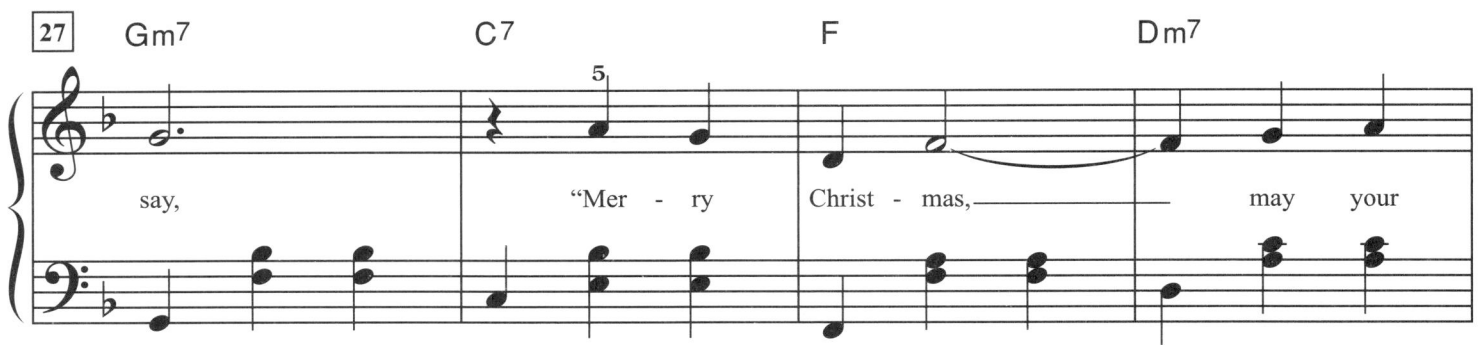
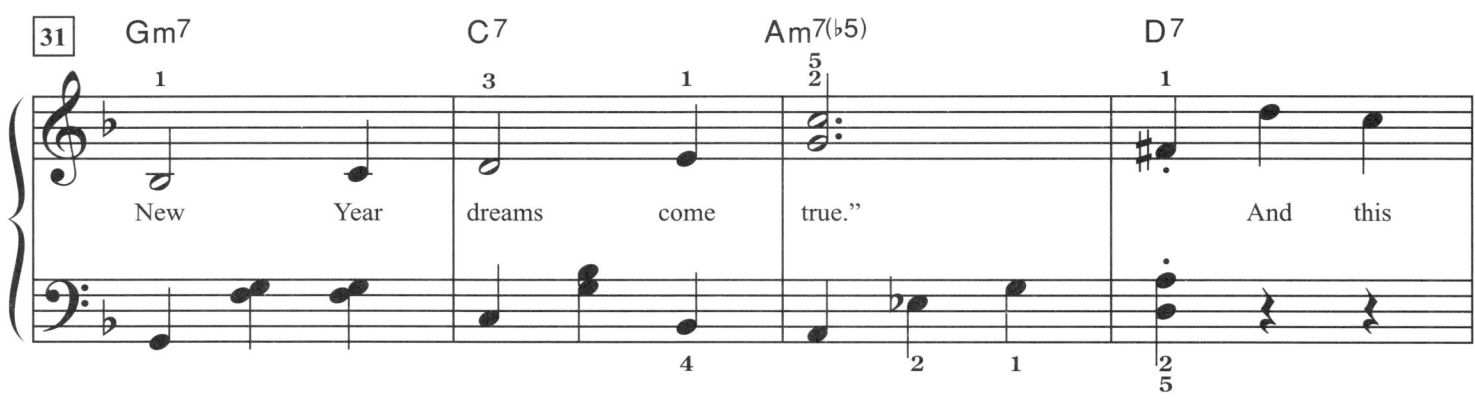
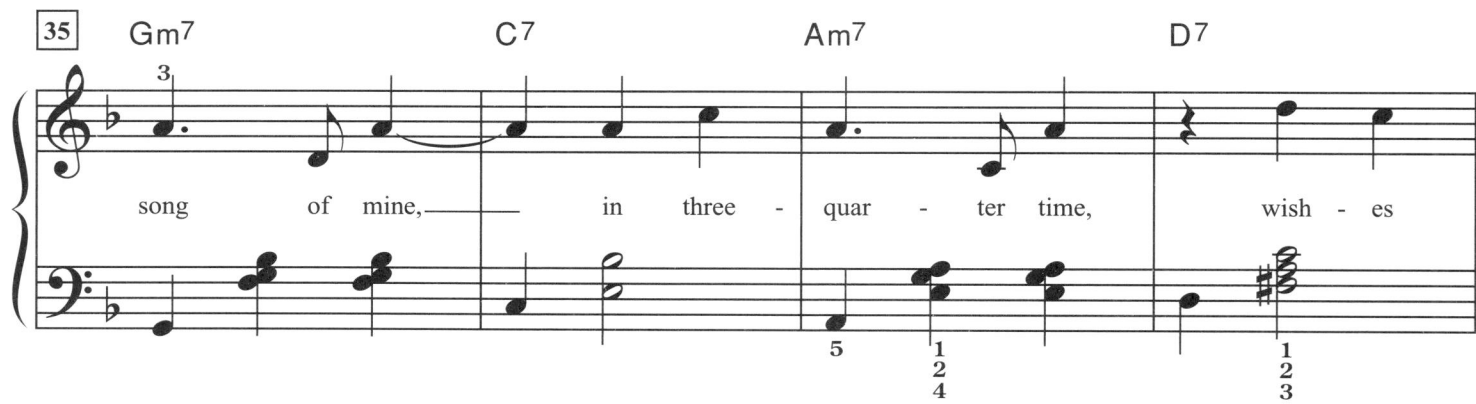
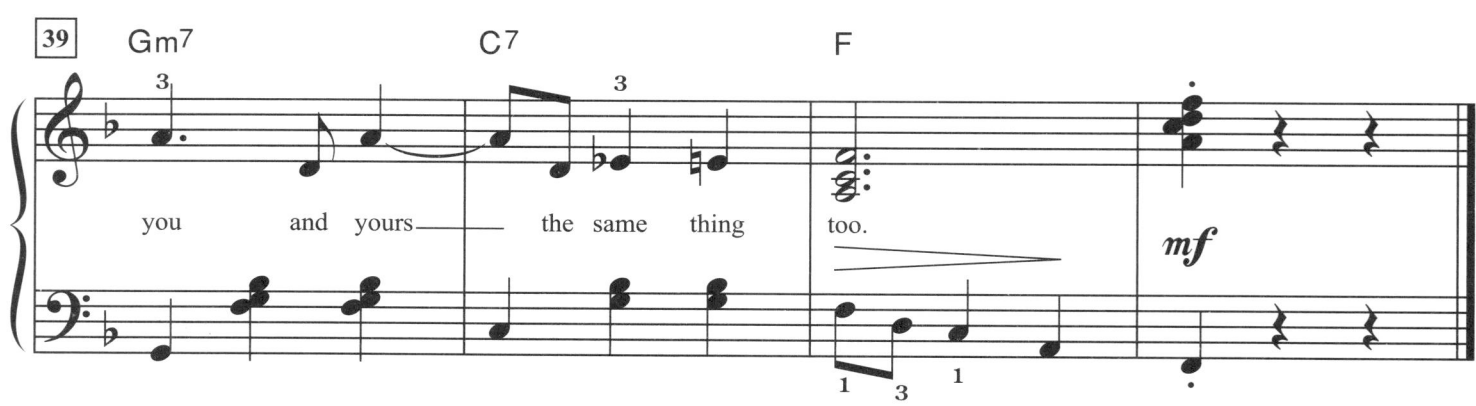

FROSTY THE SNOWMAN

Words and Music by
Steve Nelson and Jack Rollins
Arranged by Dan Coates

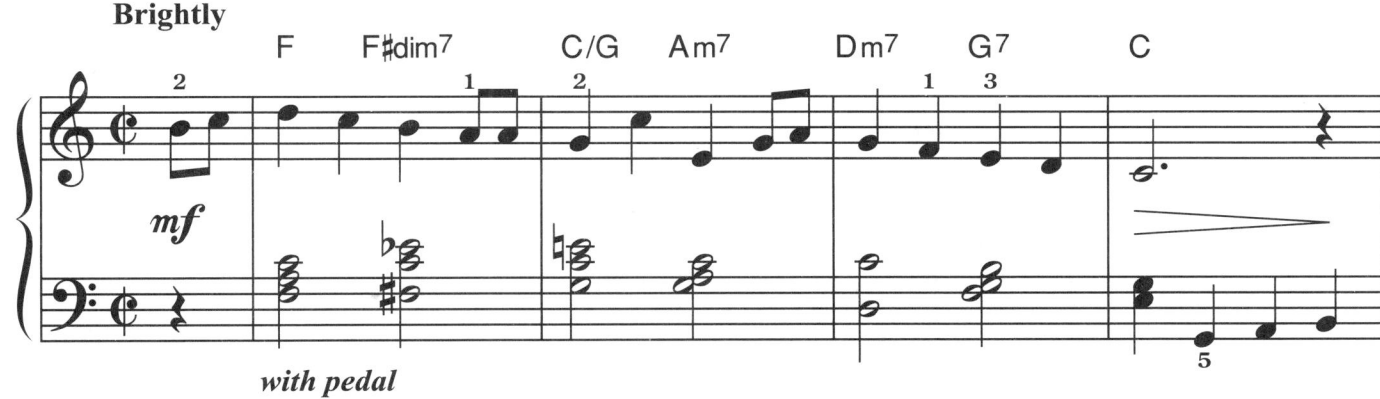

1. Frost-y the Snow-man was a jol-ly hap-py soul, with a
2. Frost-y the Snow-man knew the sun was hot that day, so he

corn-cob pipe and a but-ton nose and two eyes made out of coal.
said, "Let's run and we'll have some fun now be-fore I melt a-way."

© 1950 by HILL AND RANGE SONGS, INC.
Copyright Renewed and assigned to CHAPPELL & CO.
All Rights Reserved

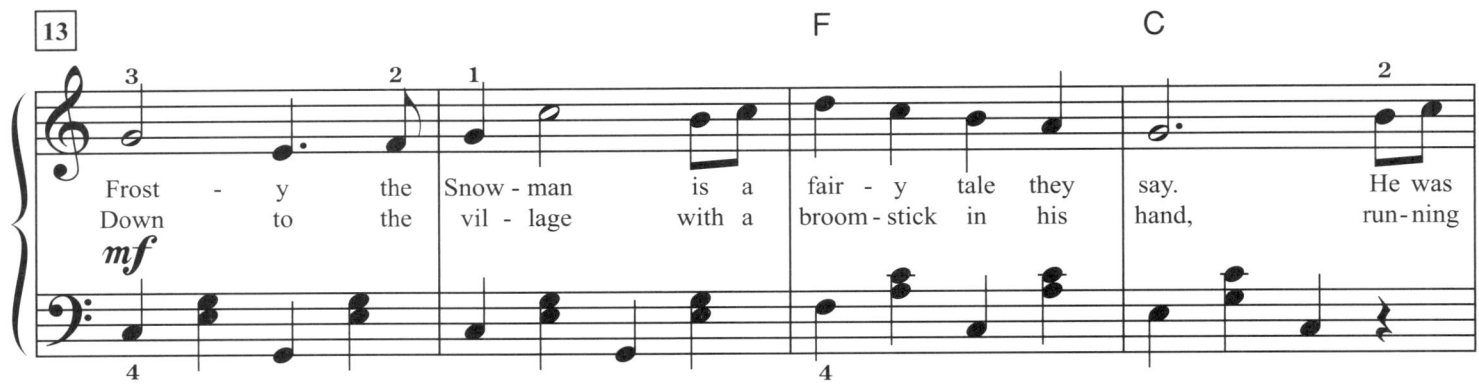
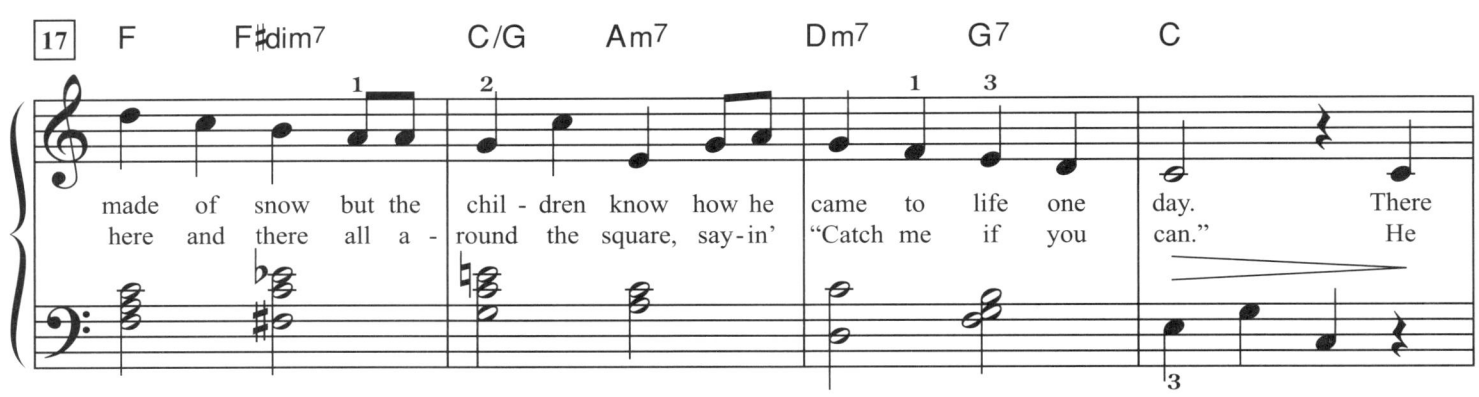
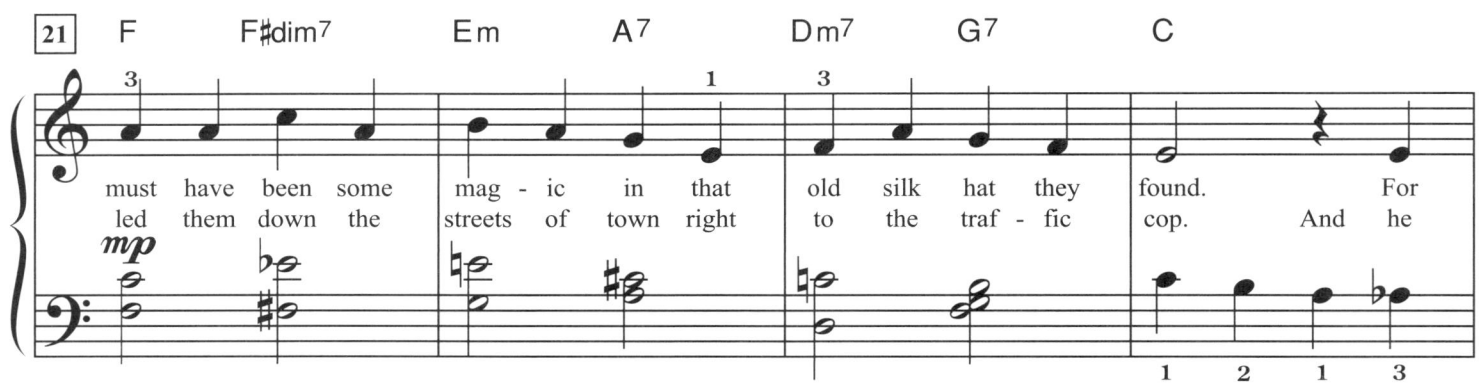
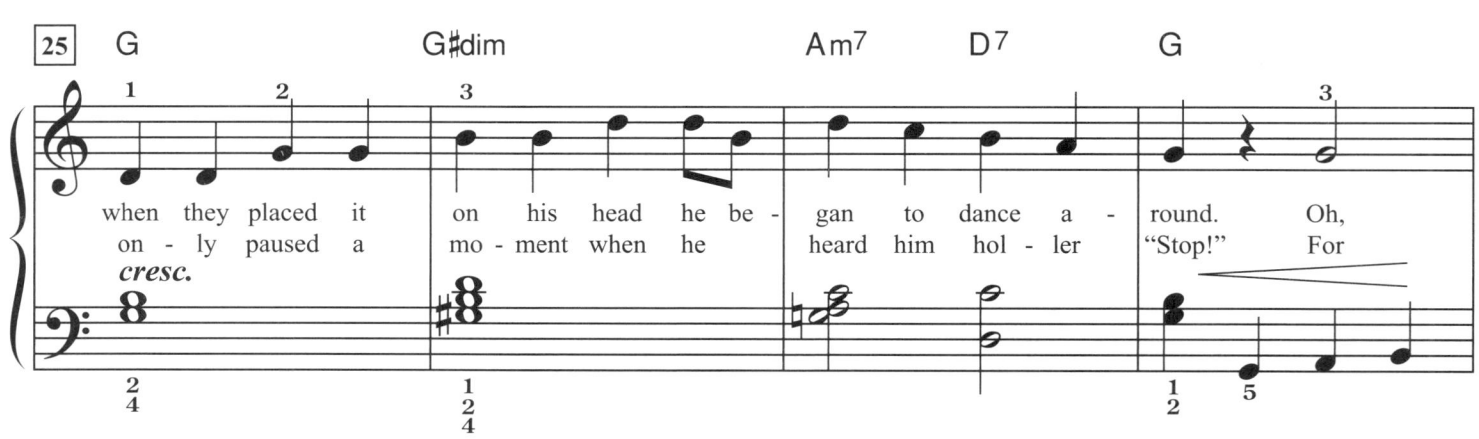

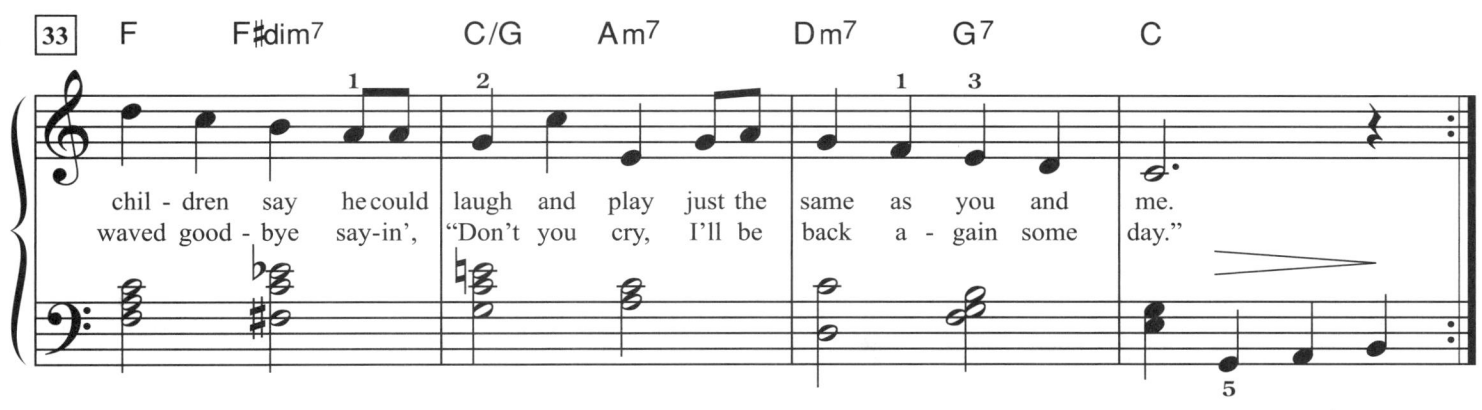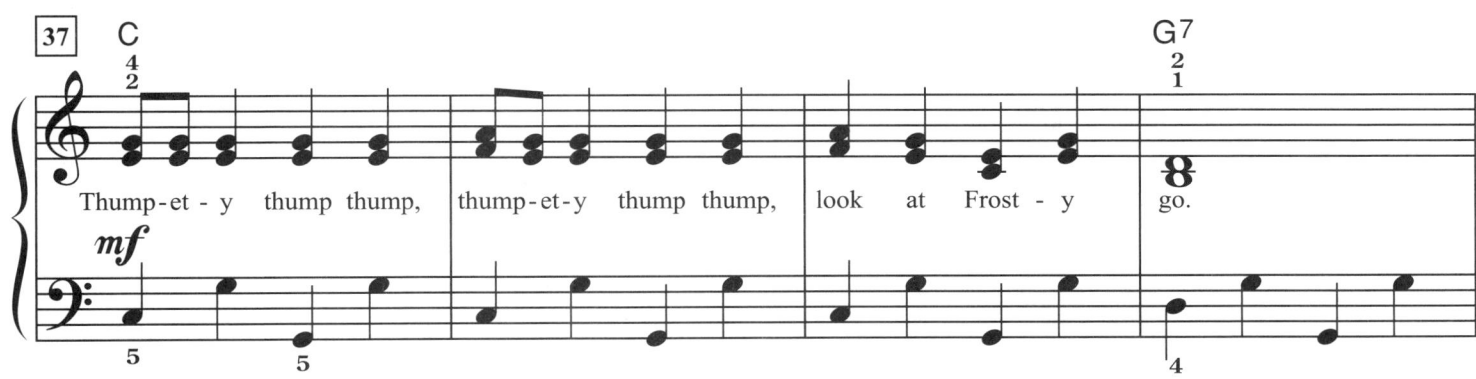

LET IT SNOW! LET IT SNOW! LET IT SNOW!

Words by Sammy Cahn
Music by Jule Styne
Arranged by Dan Coates

© 1945 (Renewed) PRODUCERS MUSIC PUBL. CO., INC. and CAHN MUSIC CO.
All Rights on Behalf of PRODUCERS MUSIC PUBL. CO., INC. Administered by CHAPPELL & CO., INC.
All Rights Reserved

HAVE YOURSELF A MERRY LITTLE CHRISTMAS

Words and Music by
Hugh Martin and Ralph Blane
Arranged by Dan Coates

© 1943 (Renewed) METRO-GOLDWYN-MAYER INC. © 1944 (Renewed) EMI FEIST CATALOG INC.
All Rights Controlled by EMI FEIST CATALOG INC. (Publishing) and ALFRED PUBLISHING CO., INC. (Print)
All Rights Reserved

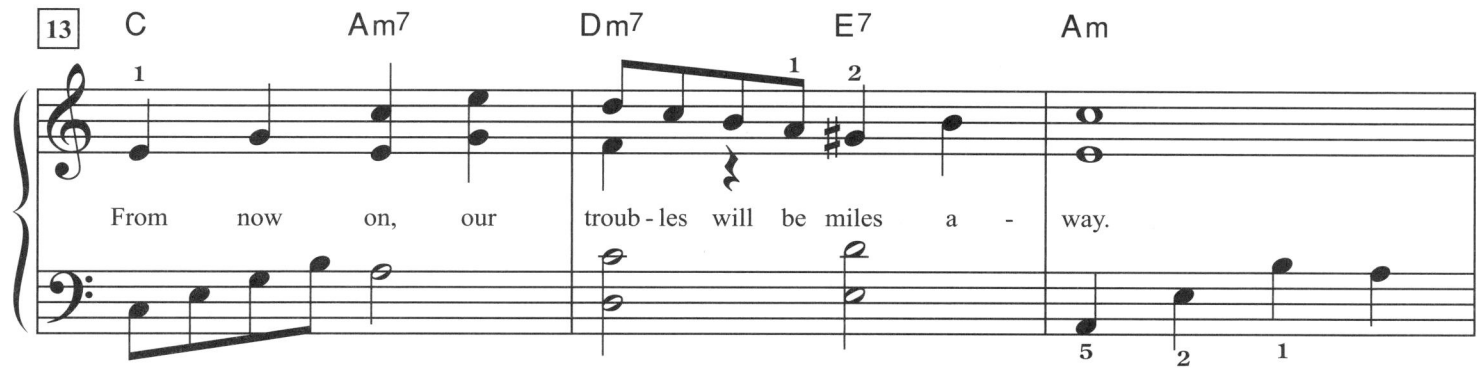
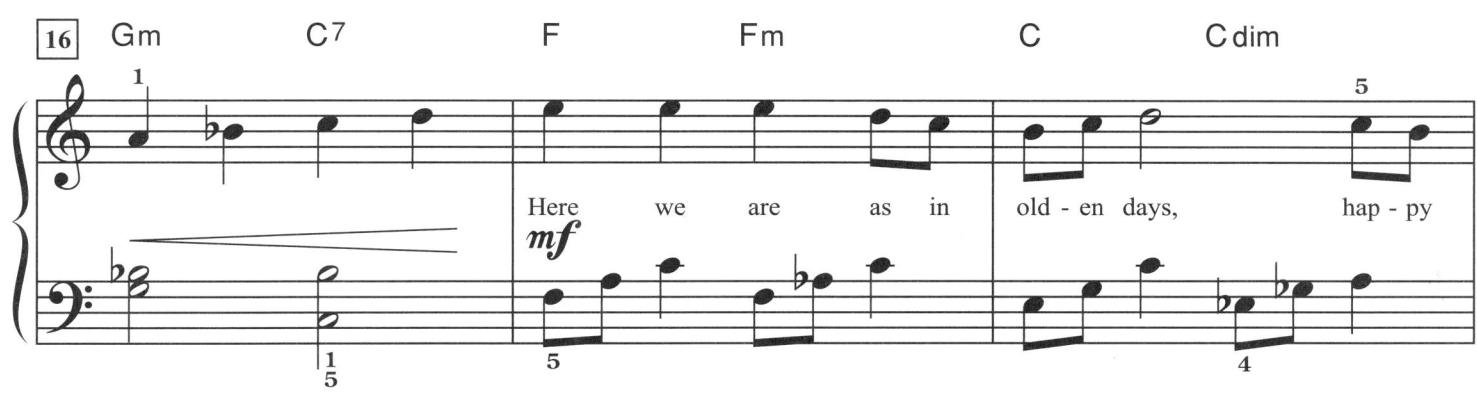
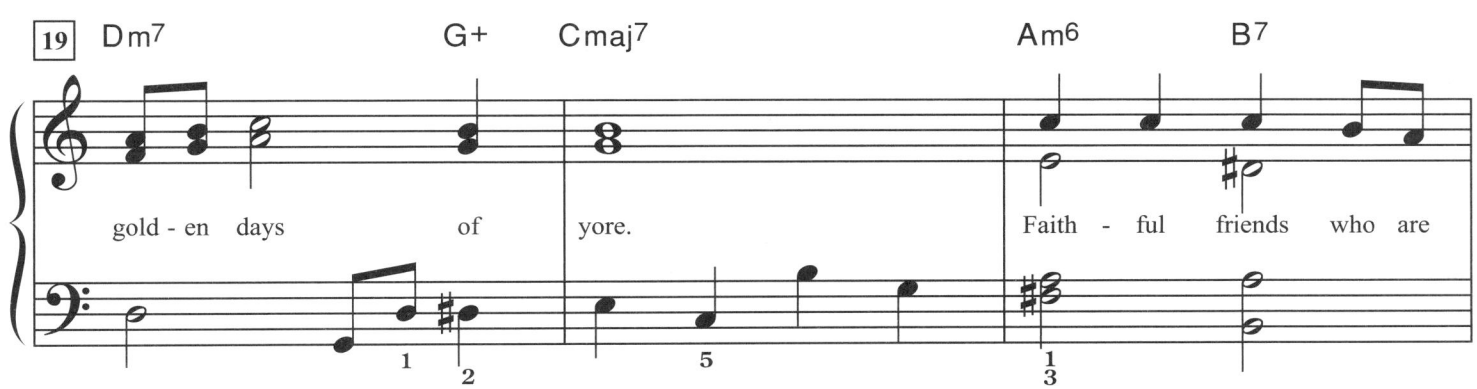
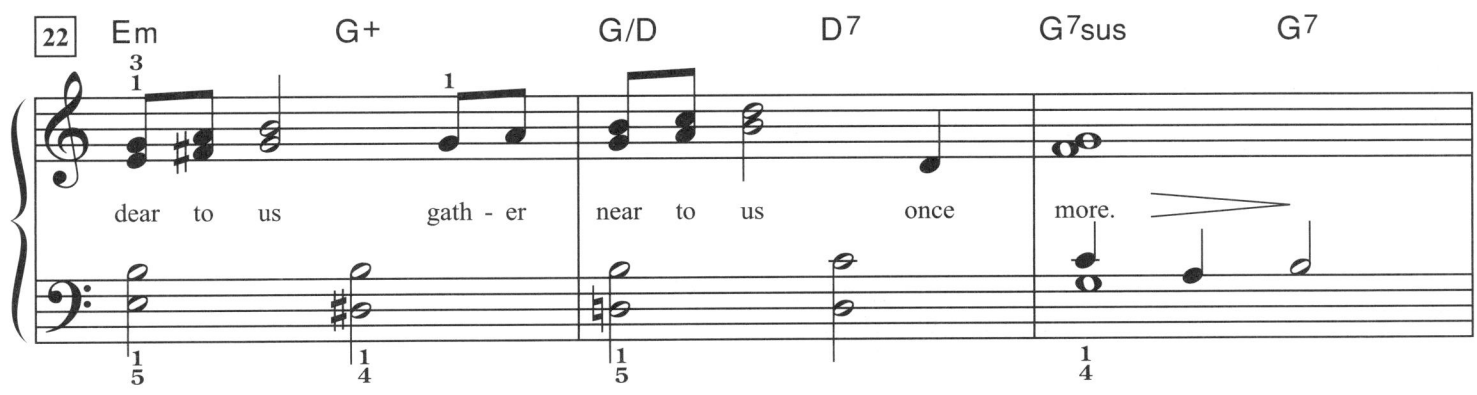

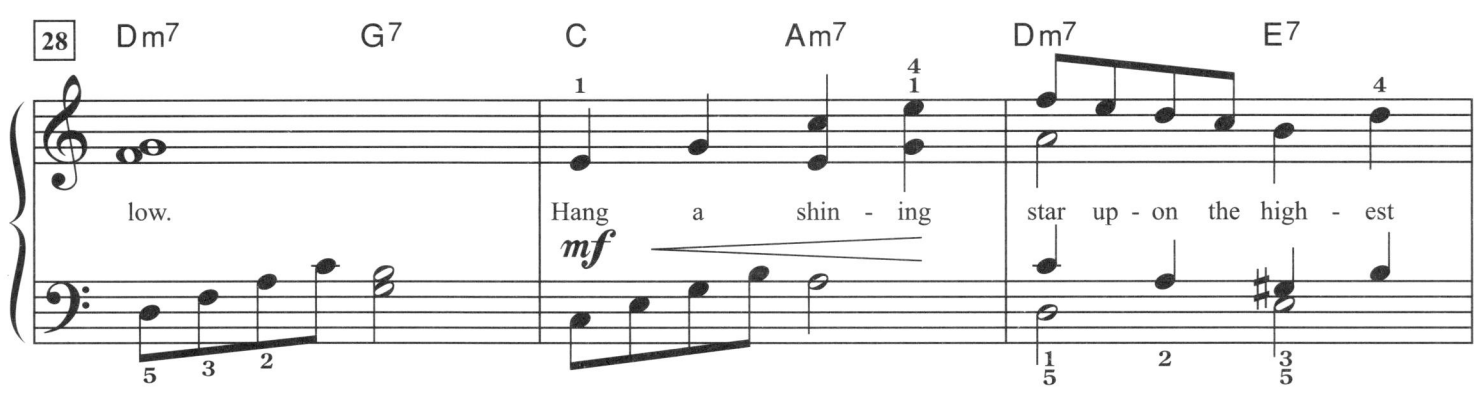
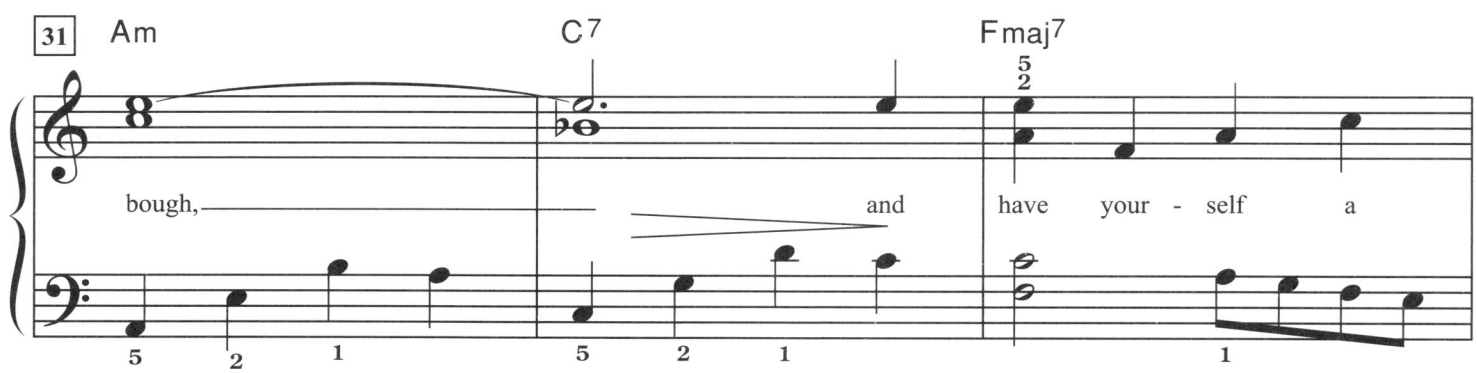

I'LL BE HOME FOR CHRISTMAS

Words by Kim Gannon
Music by Walter Kent
Arranged by Dan Coates

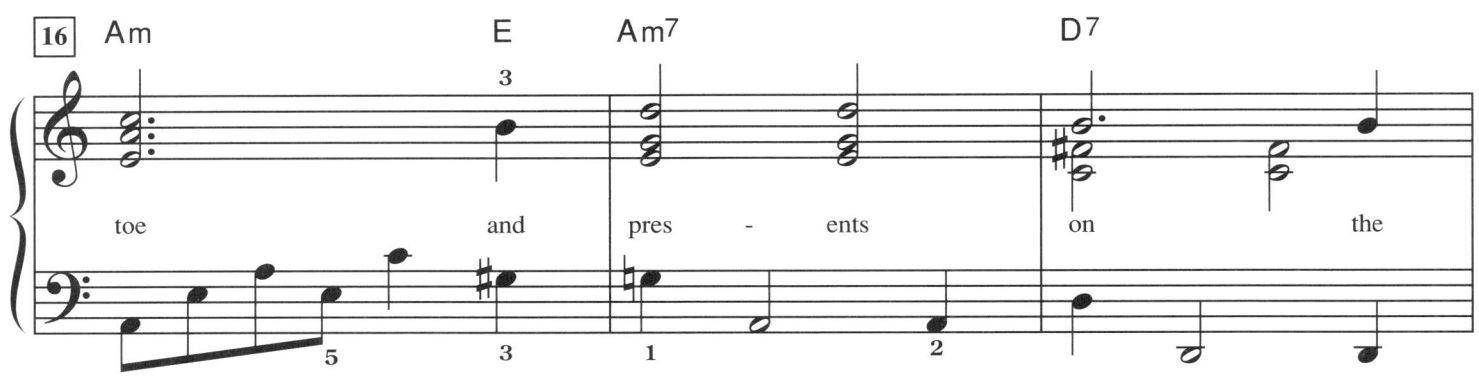

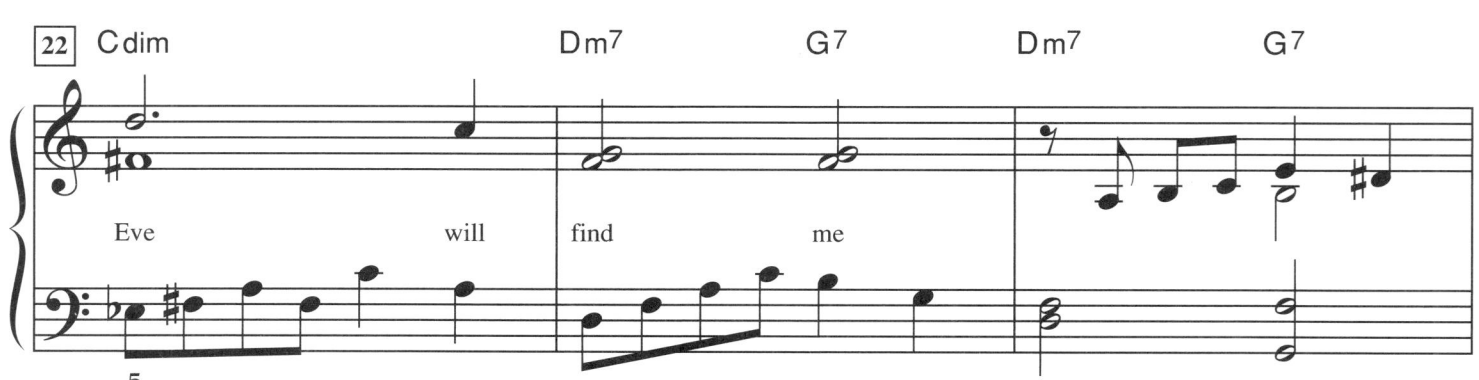

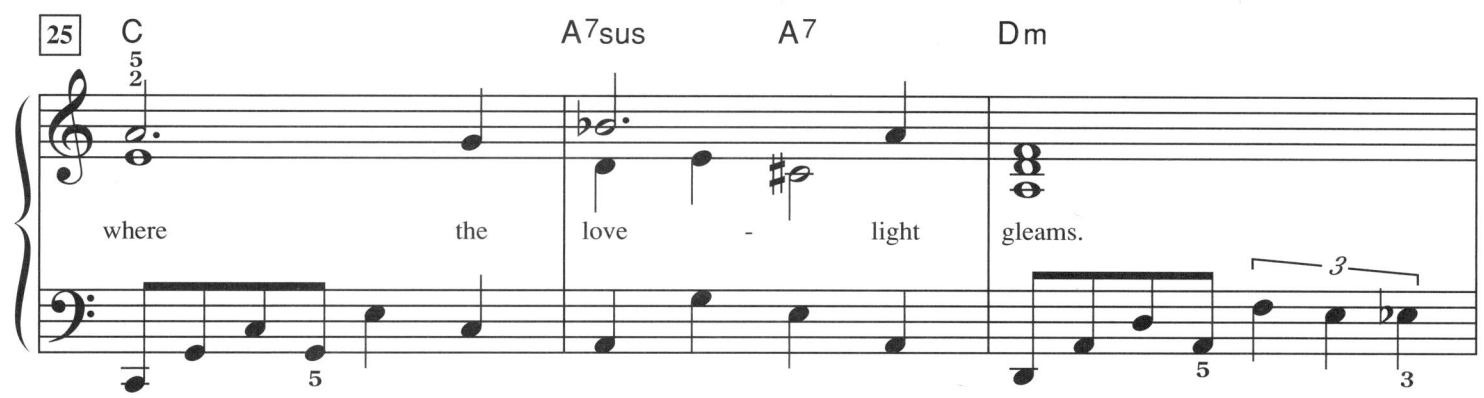
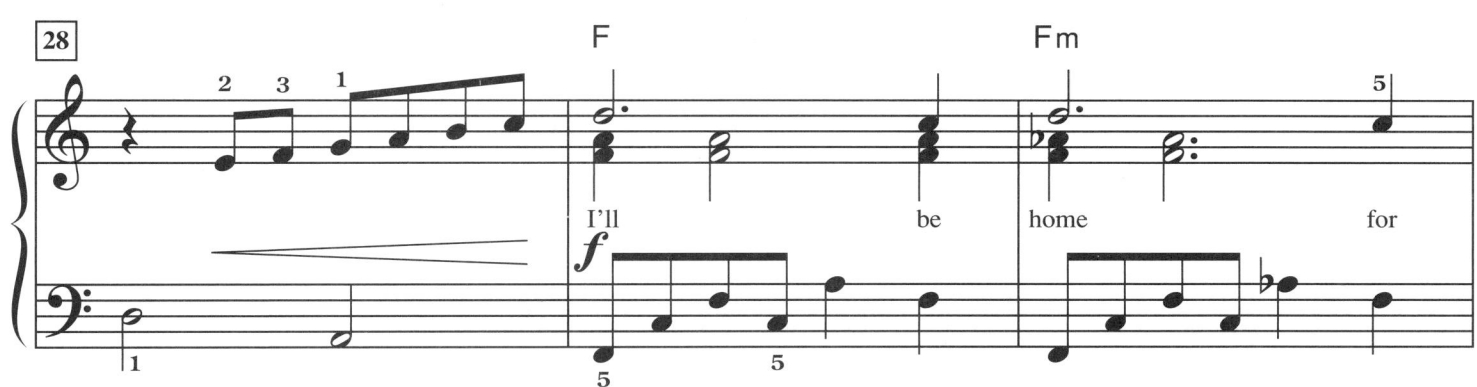
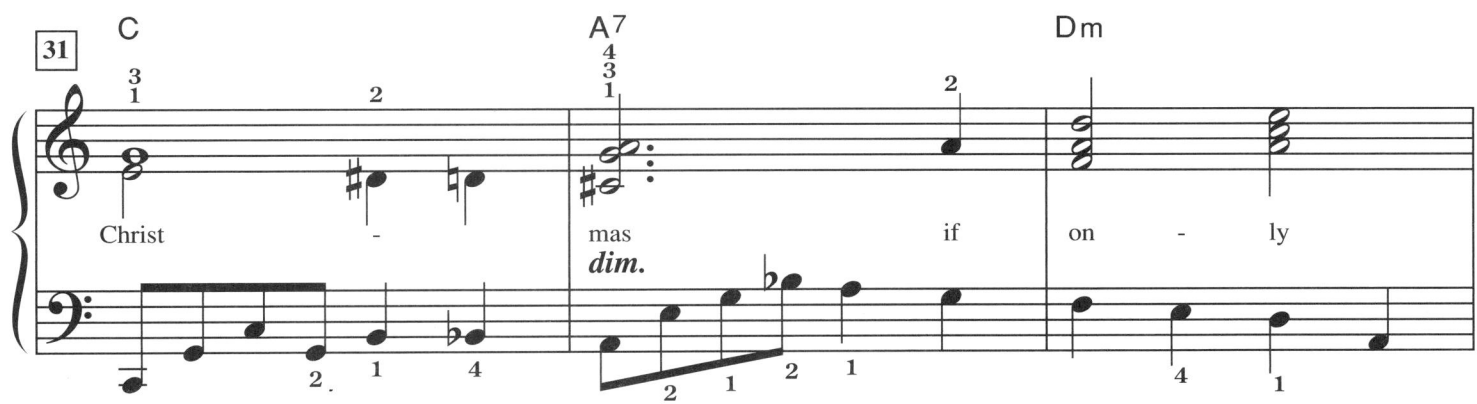

IT'S THE MOST WONDERFUL TIME OF THE YEAR

Words and Music by
Eddie Pola and George Wyle
Arranged by Dan Coates

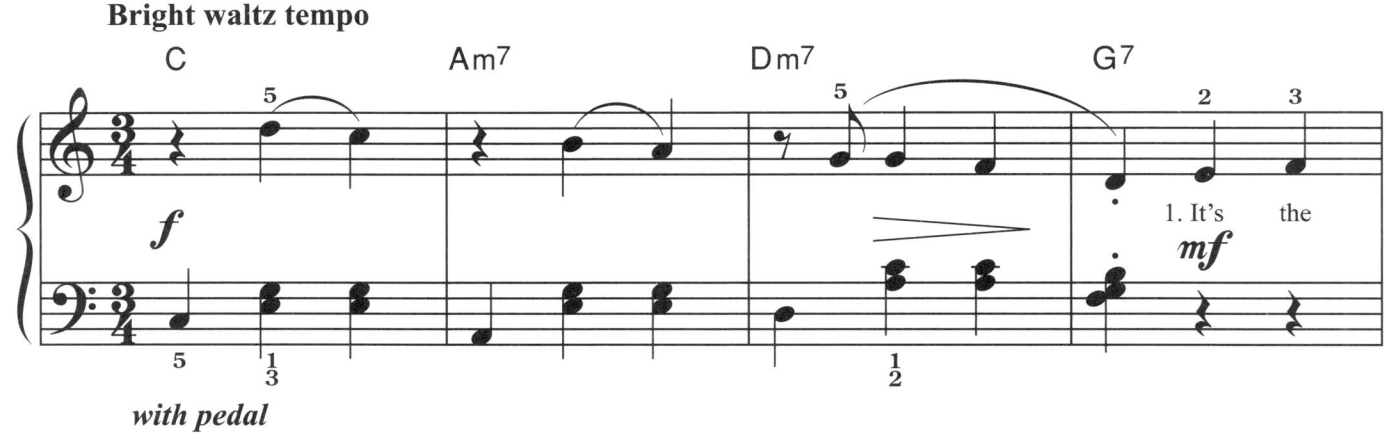

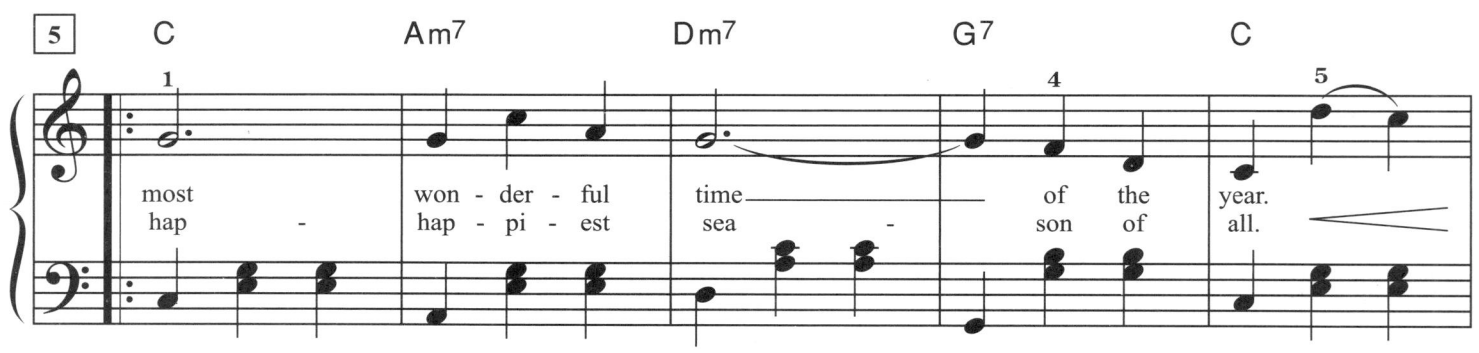

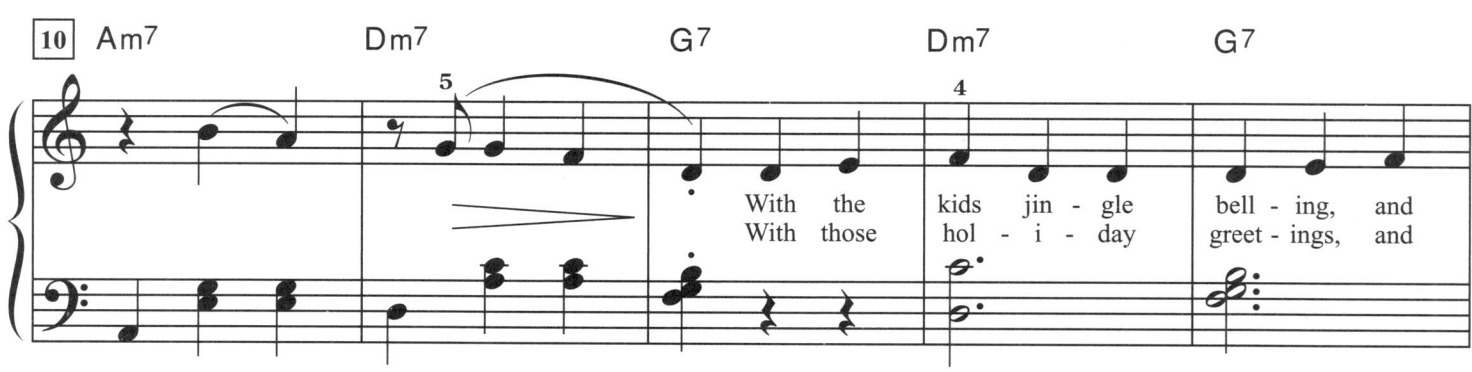

© 1963 (Renewed) BARNABY MUSIC CORP.
All Rights Reserved

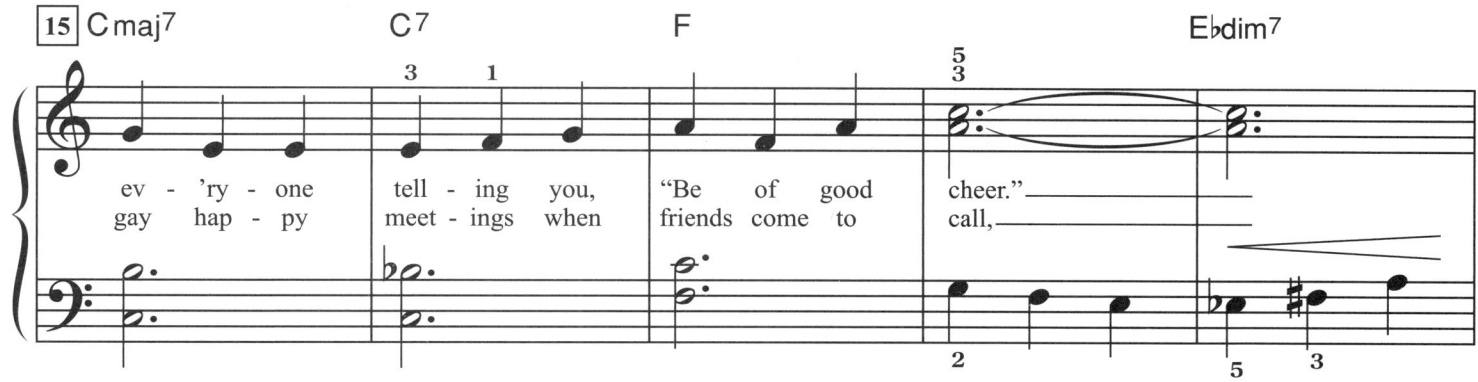
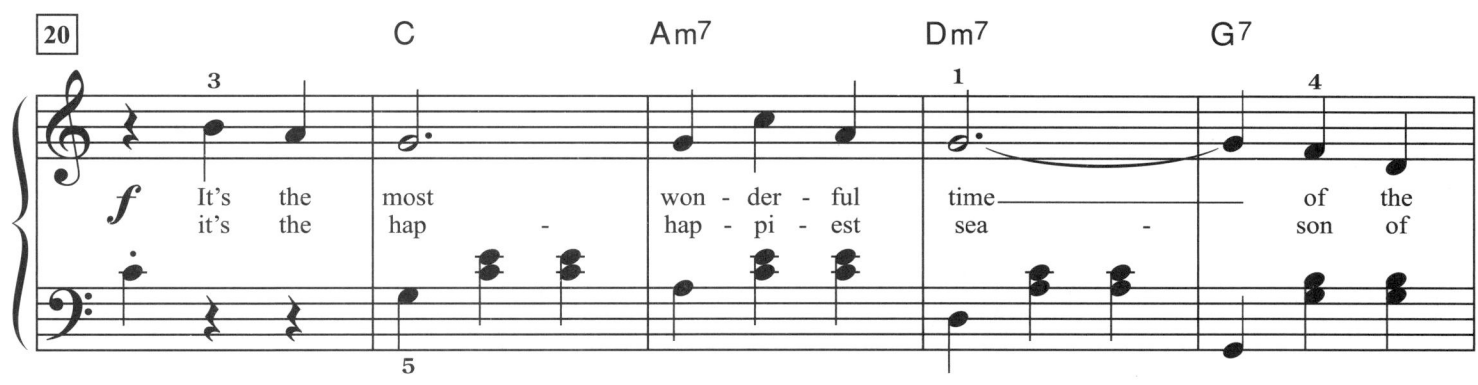
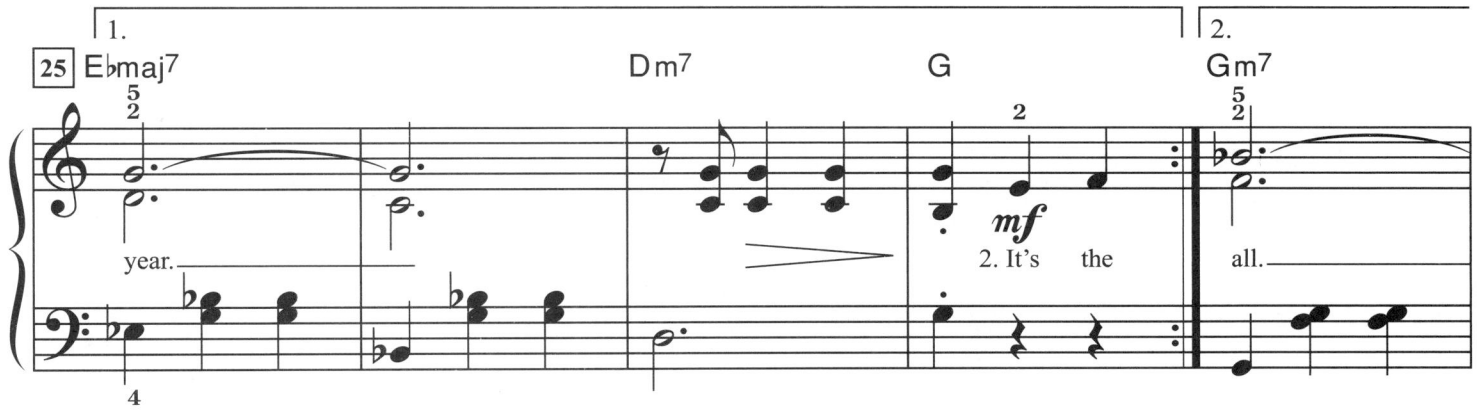

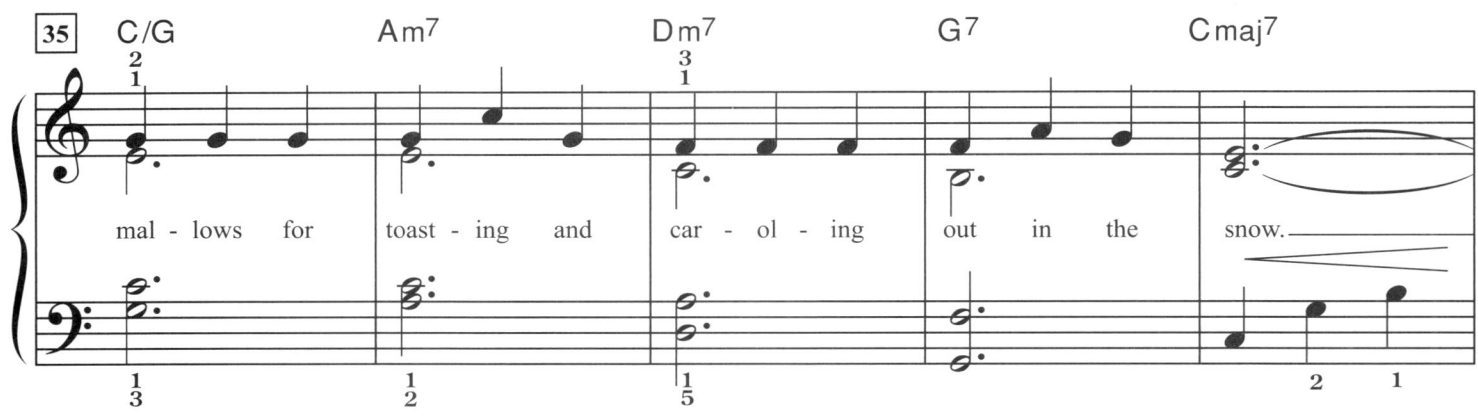
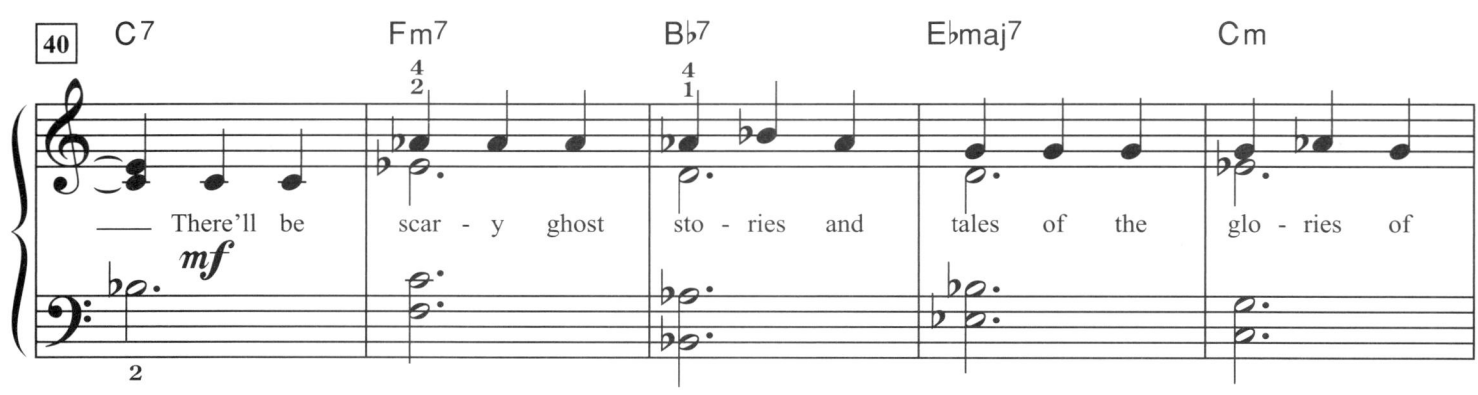
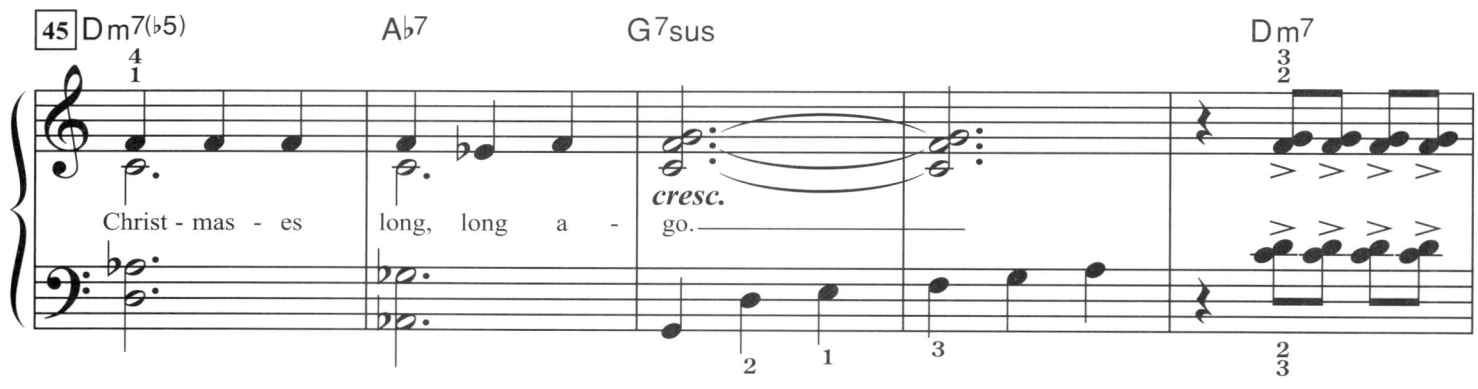

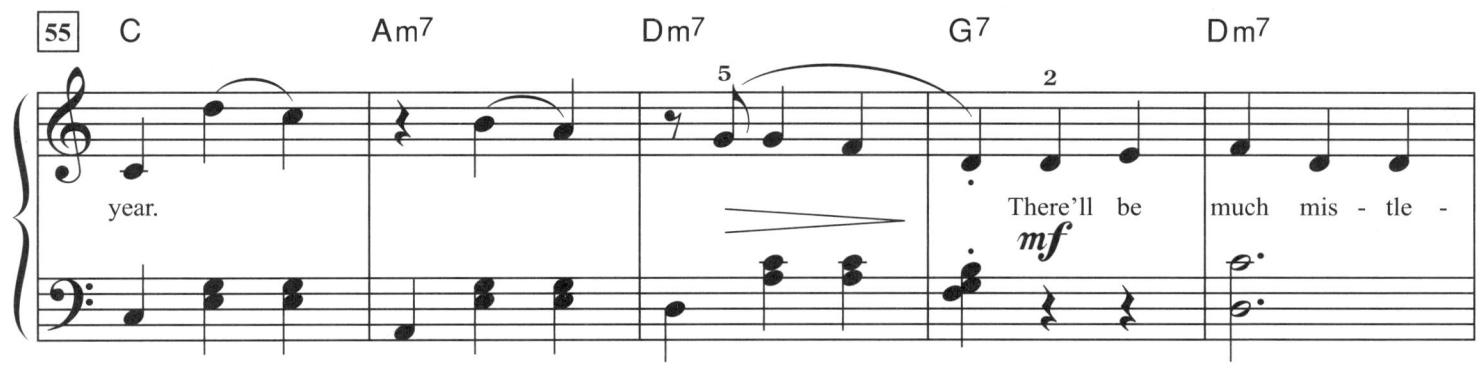
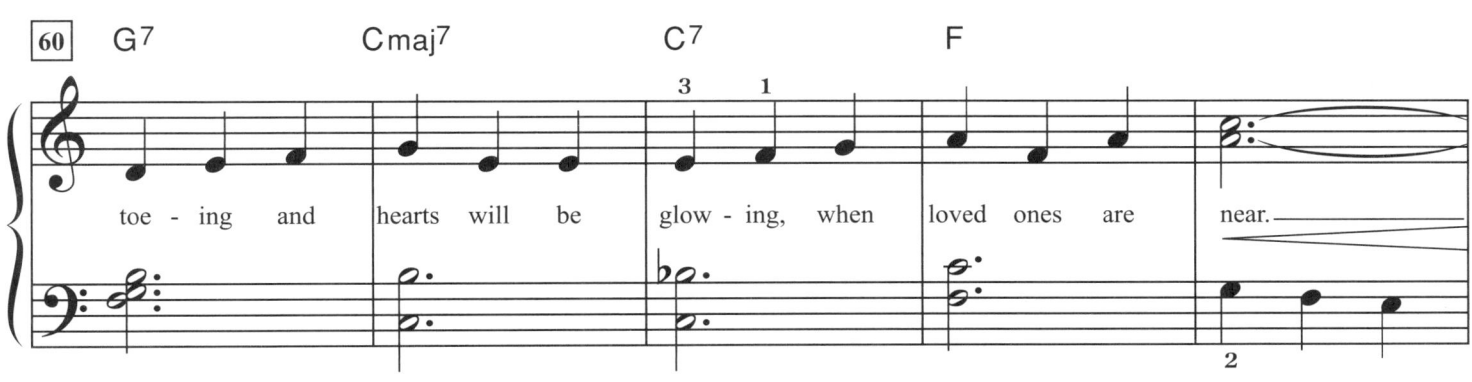
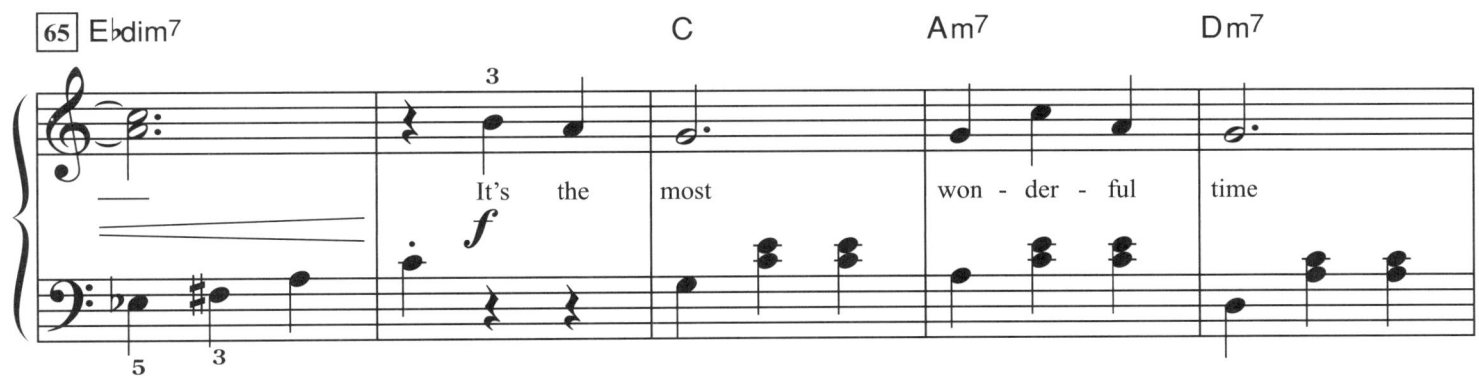
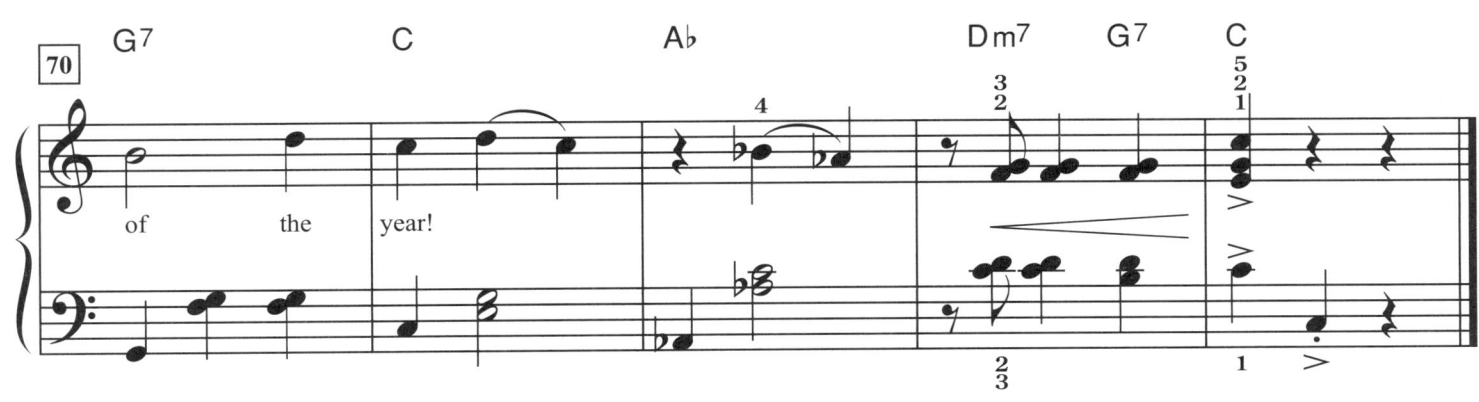

SANTA CLAUS IS COMIN' TO TOWN

Words by Haven Gillespie
Music by J. Fred Coots
Arranged by Dan Coates

© 1934 (Renewed) EMI Feist Catalog Inc.
Rights for the Extended Renewal Term in the United States Controlled by HAVEN GILLESPIE MUSIC and EMI FEIST CATALOG INC.
All Rights Controlled outside the United Stated Controlled by EMI FEIST CATALOG INC. (Publishing) and ALFRED PUBLISHING CO., INC. (Print)
All Rights Reserved

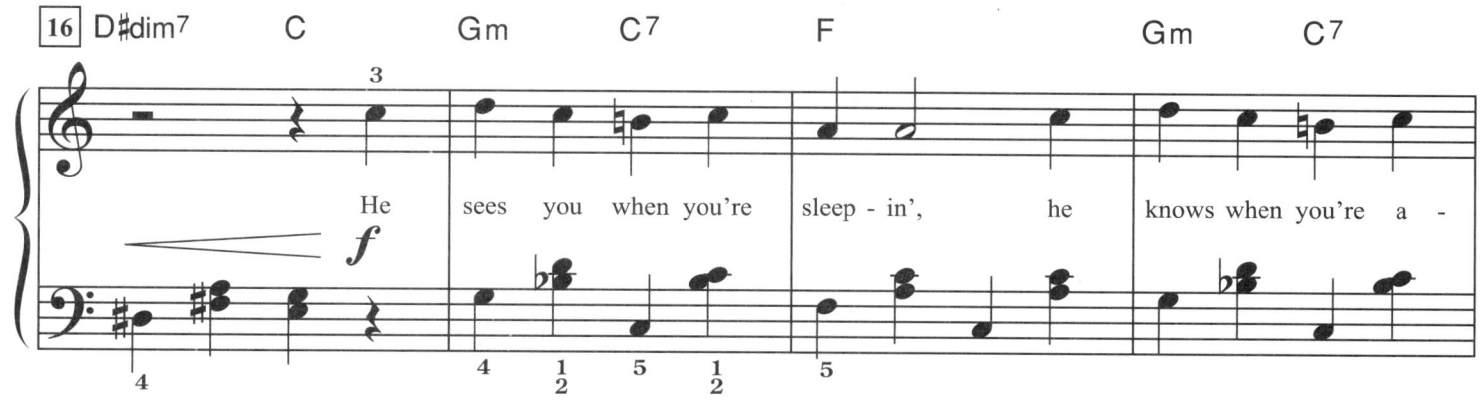
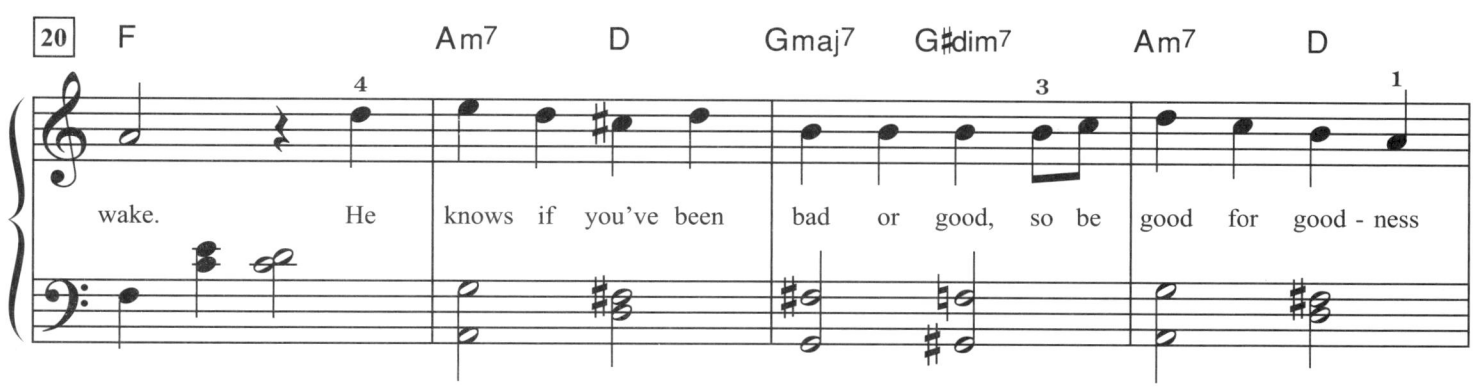
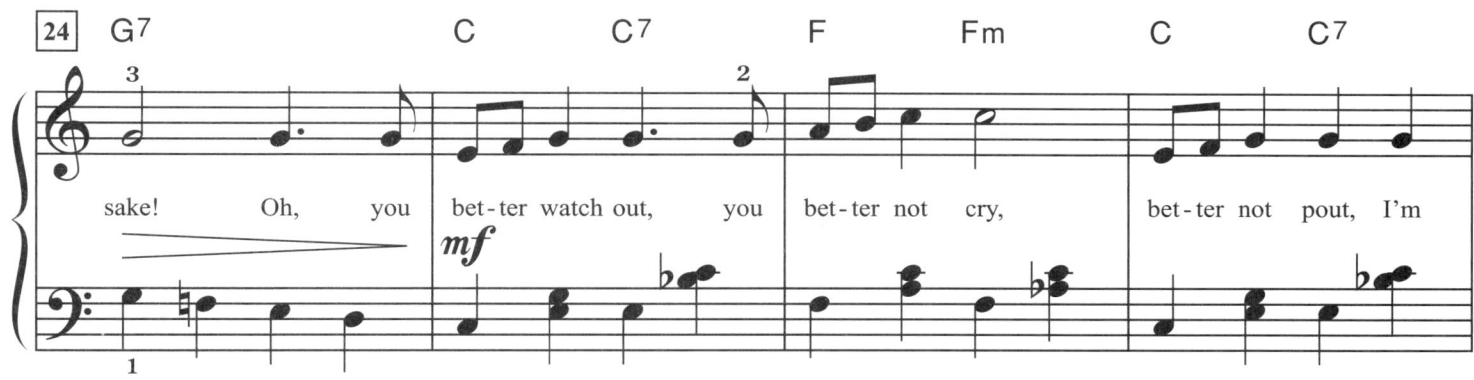
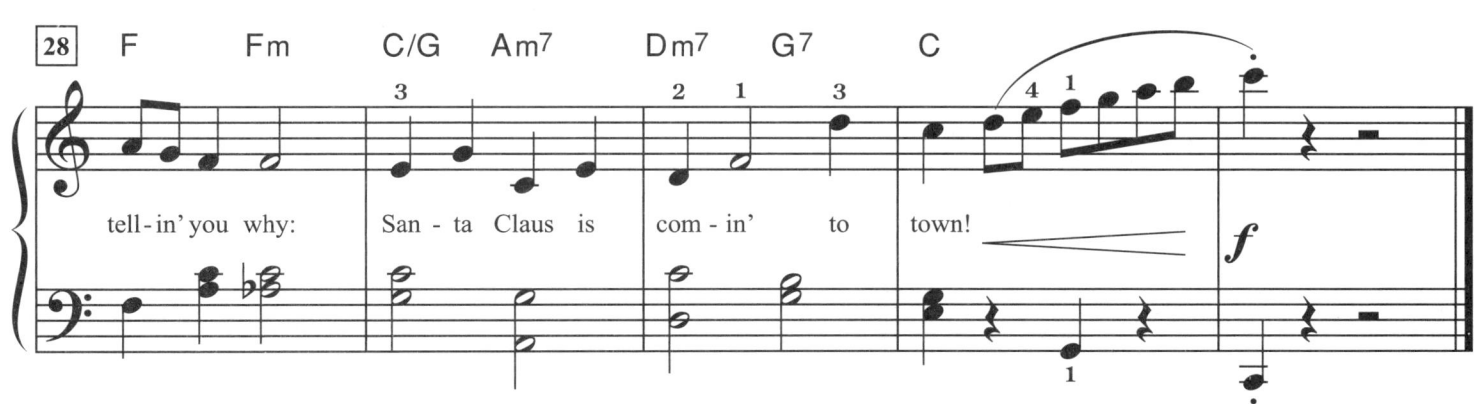

SLEIGH RIDE

By Leroy Anderson
Arranged by Dan Coates

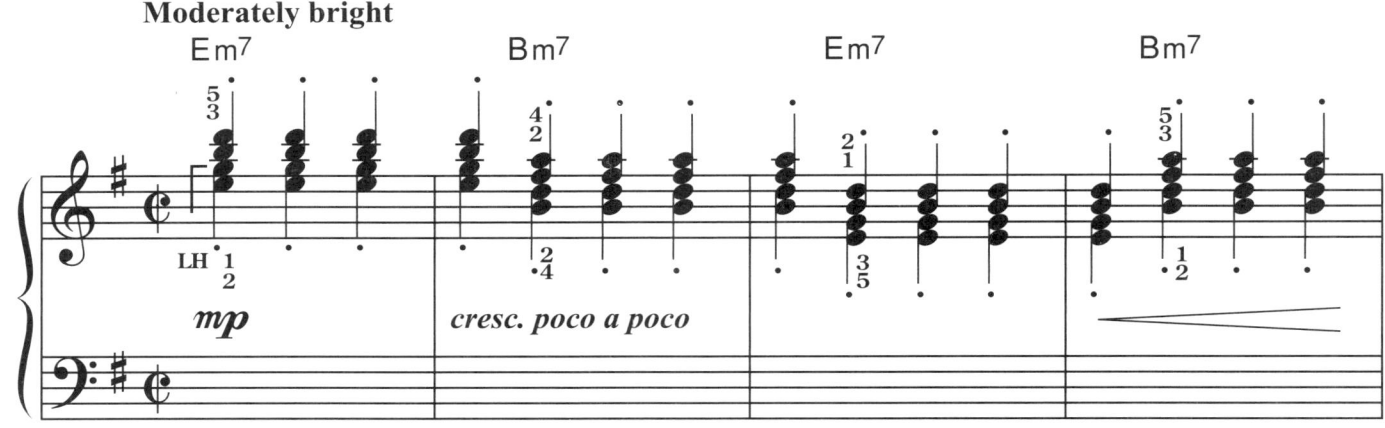

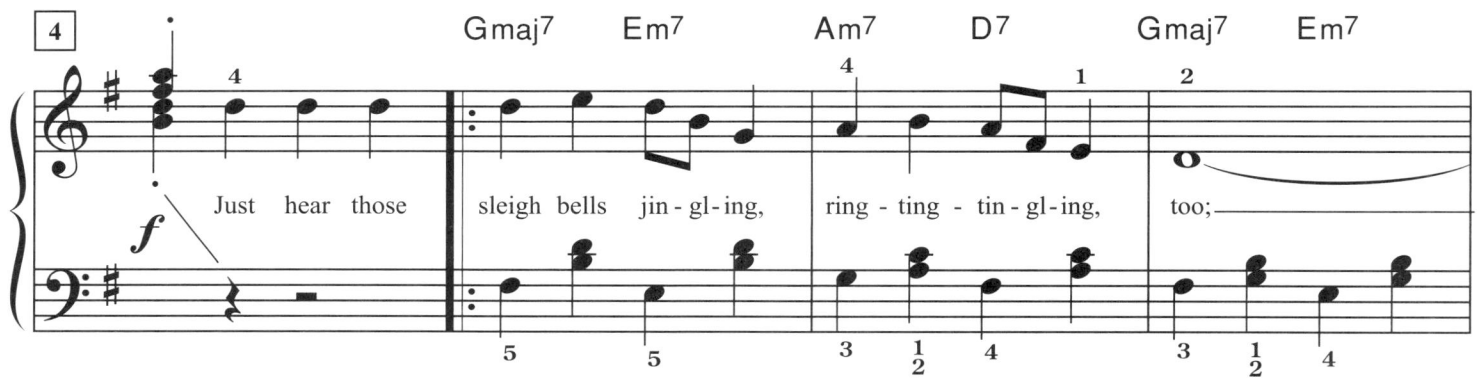

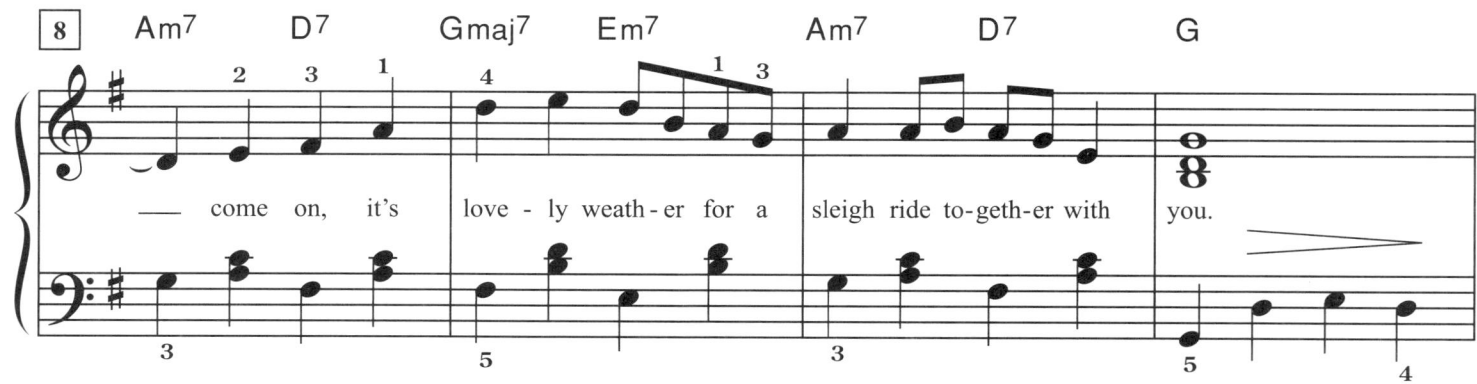

© 1948 (Renewed) EMI MILLS MUSIC, INC. Rights for the Extended Renewal Term in the U.S. Assigned to WOODBURY MUSIC COMPANY
Worldwide Print Rights Administered by ALFRED PUBLISHING CO., INC.
All Rights Reserved

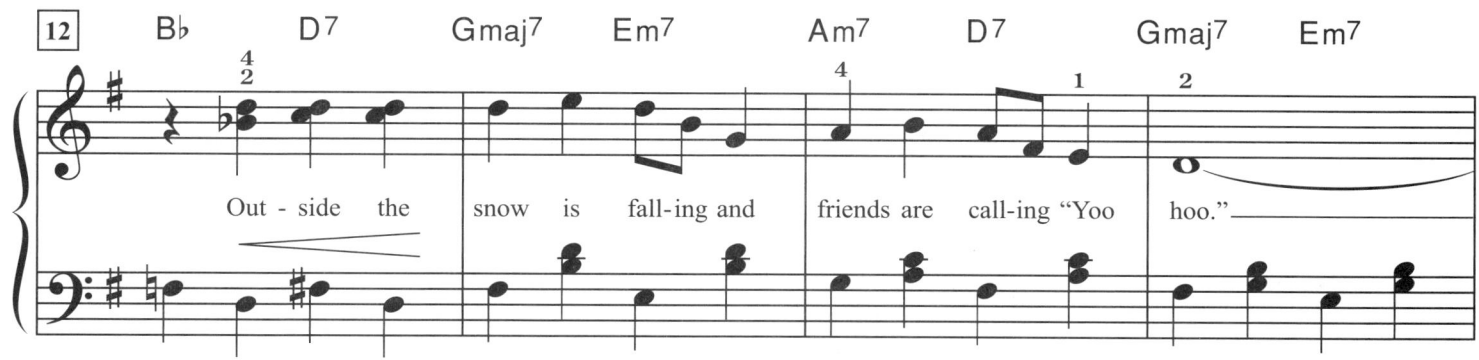
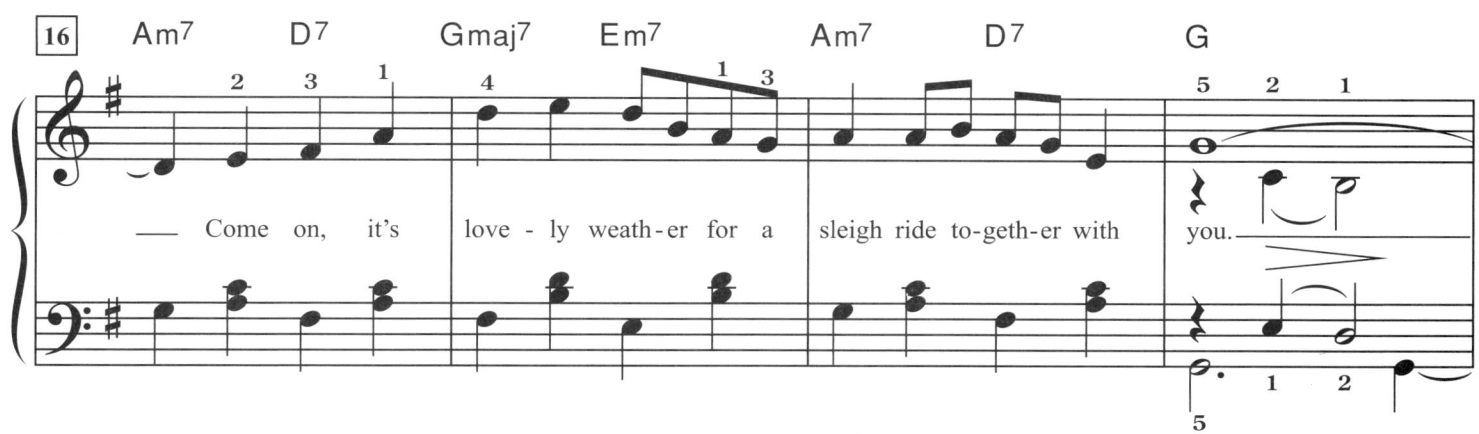

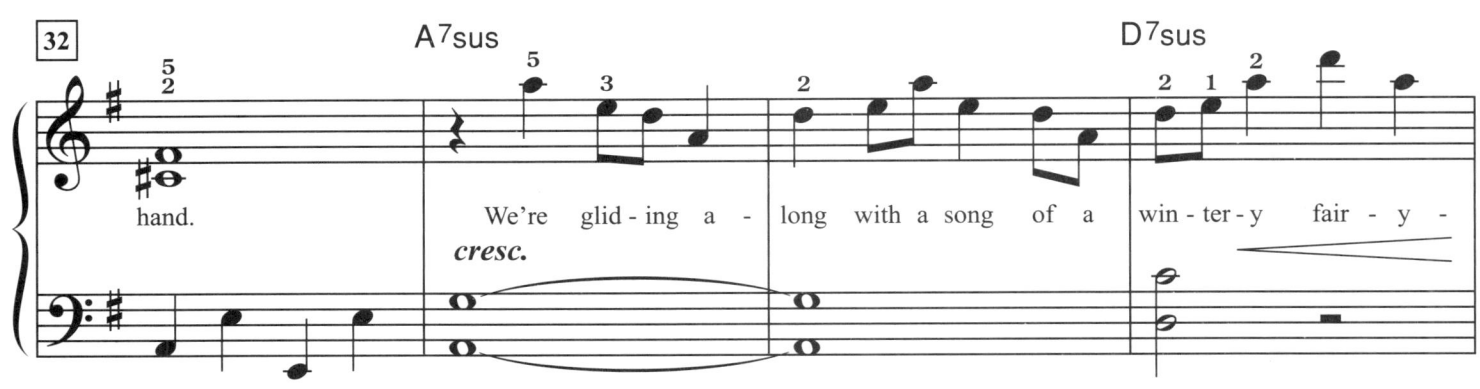
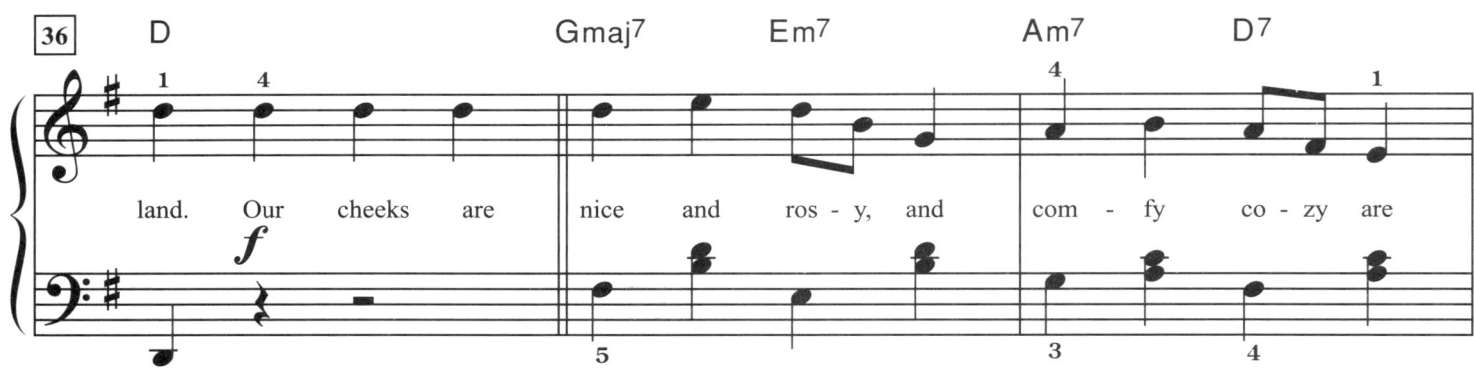
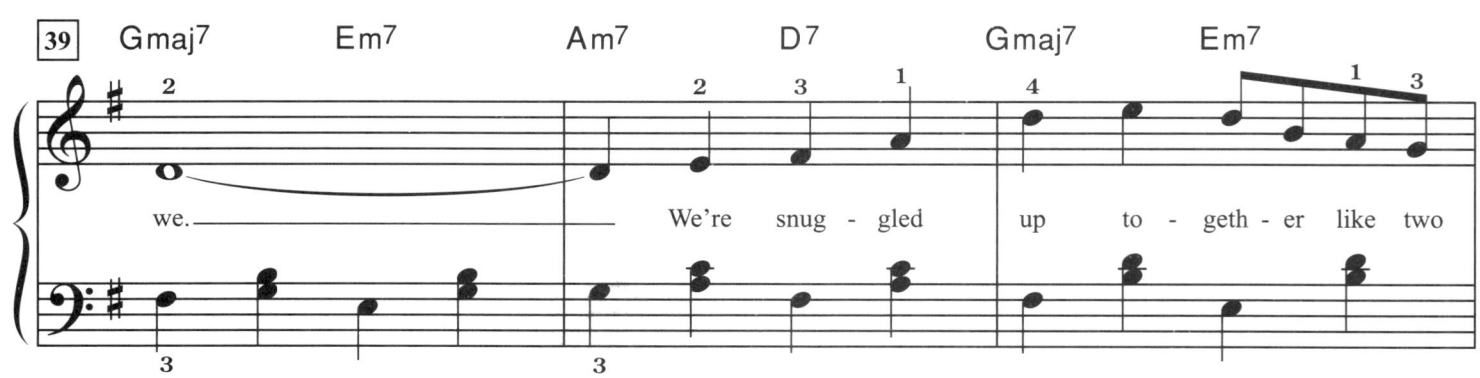

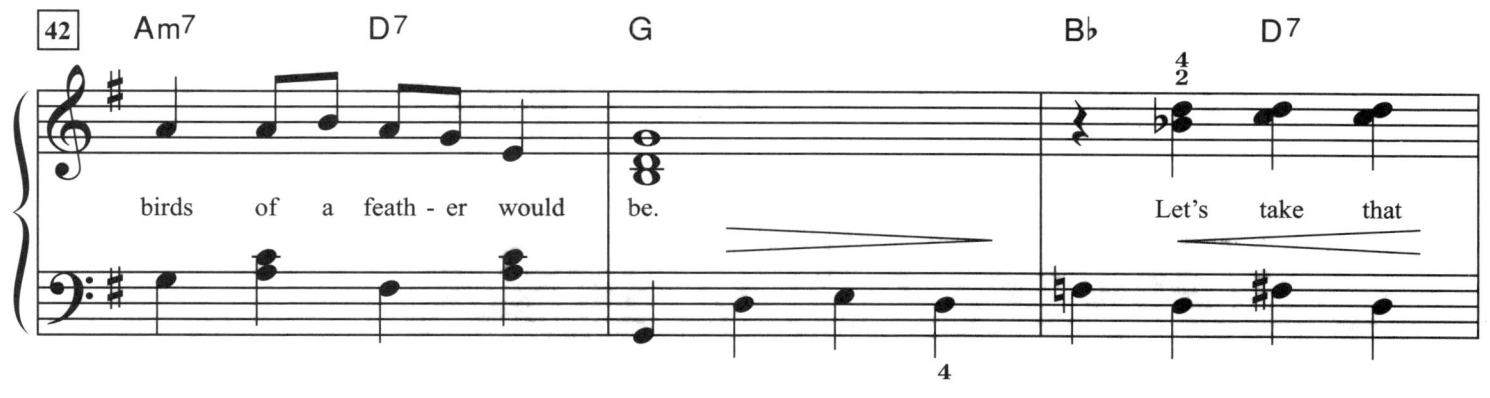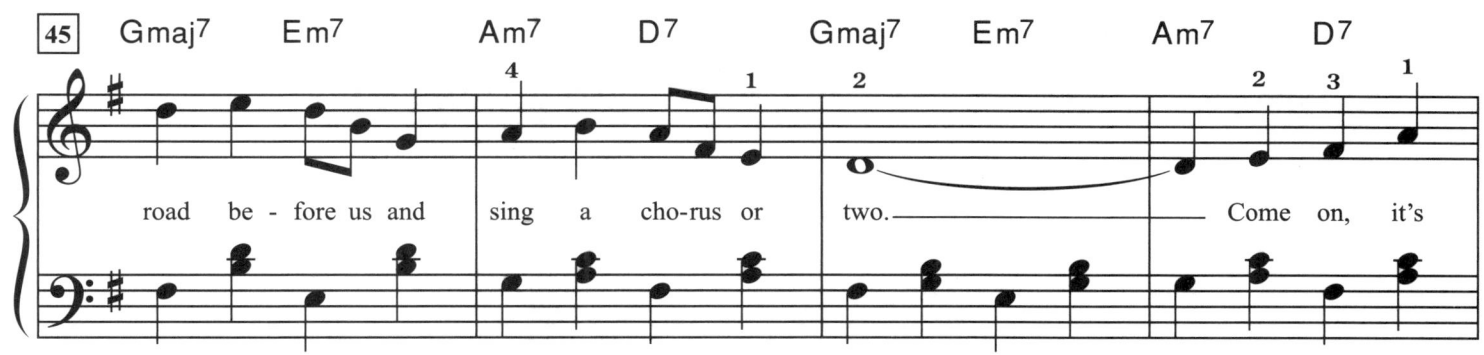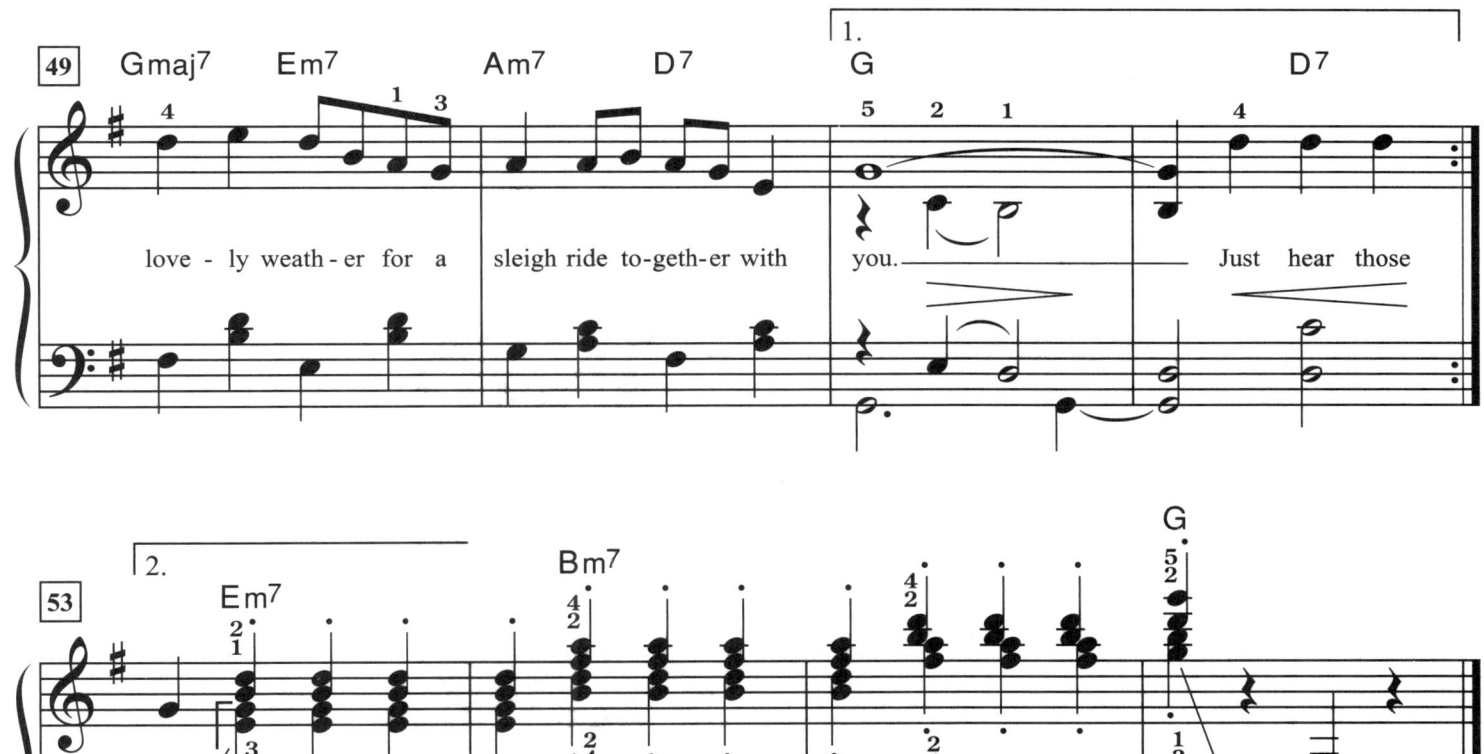

WINTER WONDERLAND

Words by Dick Smith
Music by Felix Bernard
Arranged by Dan Coates

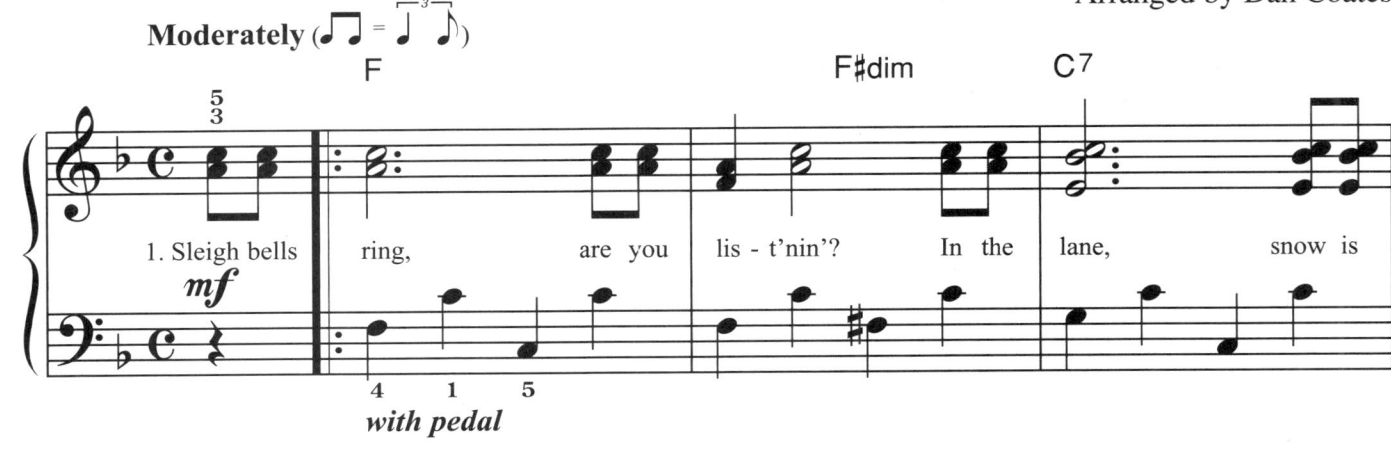

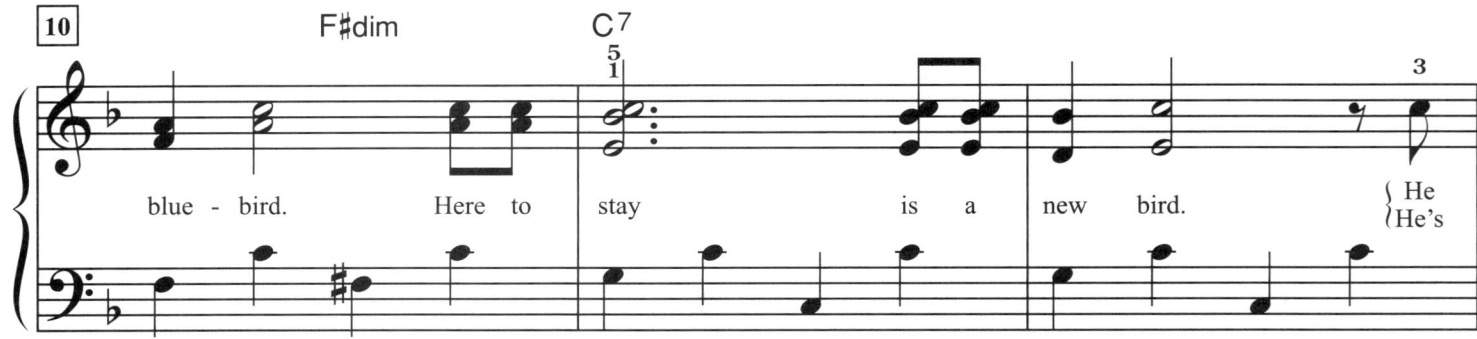

© 1934 (Renewed) WB MUSIC CORP.
All Rights Reserved

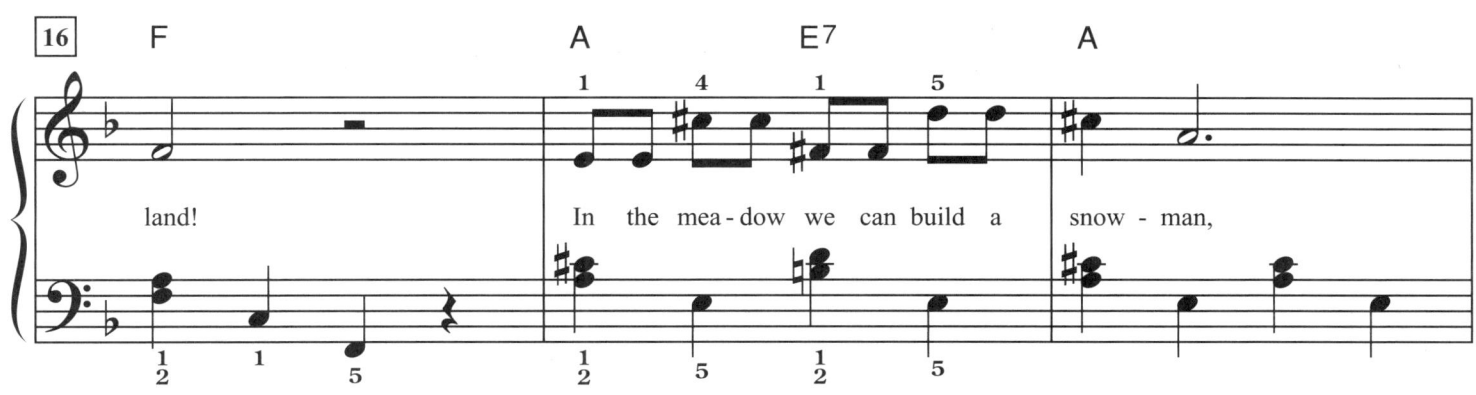
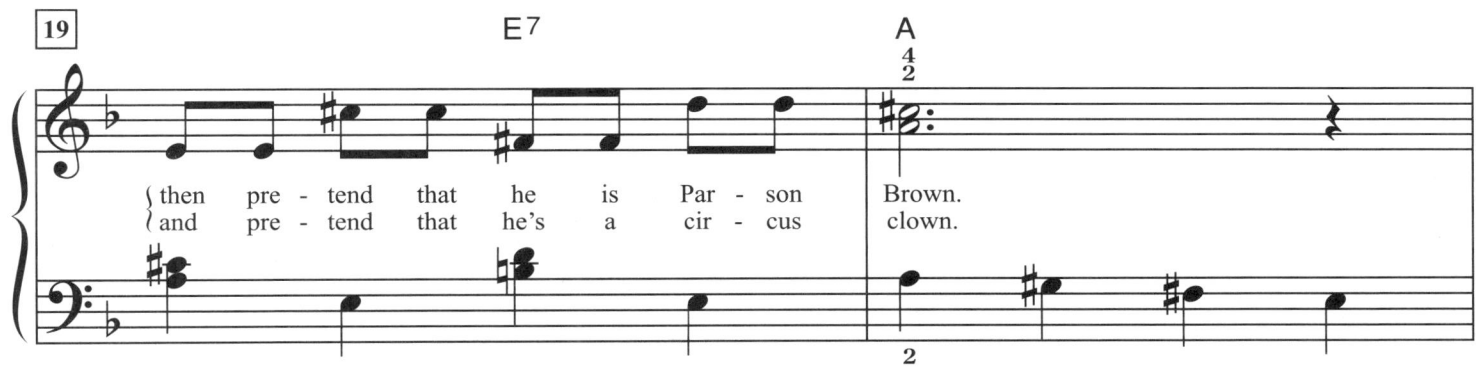
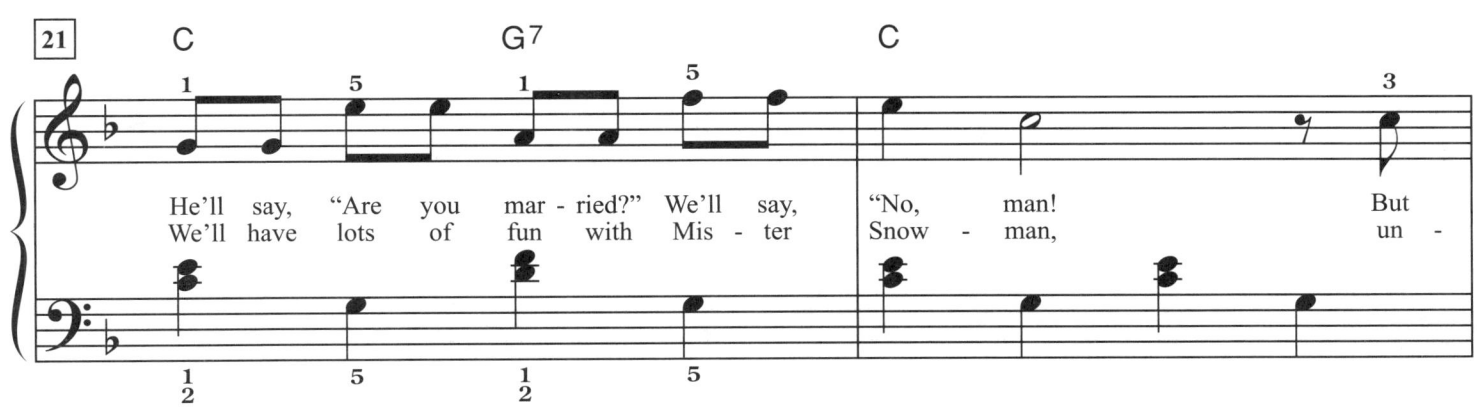

JINGLE BELL ROCK

Words and Music by
Joe Beal and Jim Boothe
Arranged by Dan Coates

© 1957 (Renewed) CHAPPELL & CO., INC.
All Rights Reserved

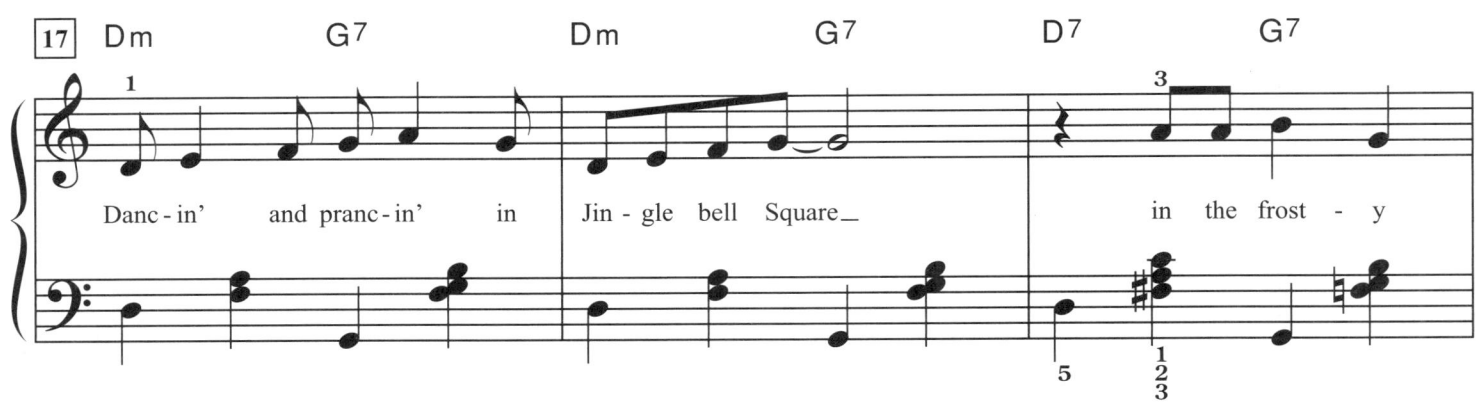

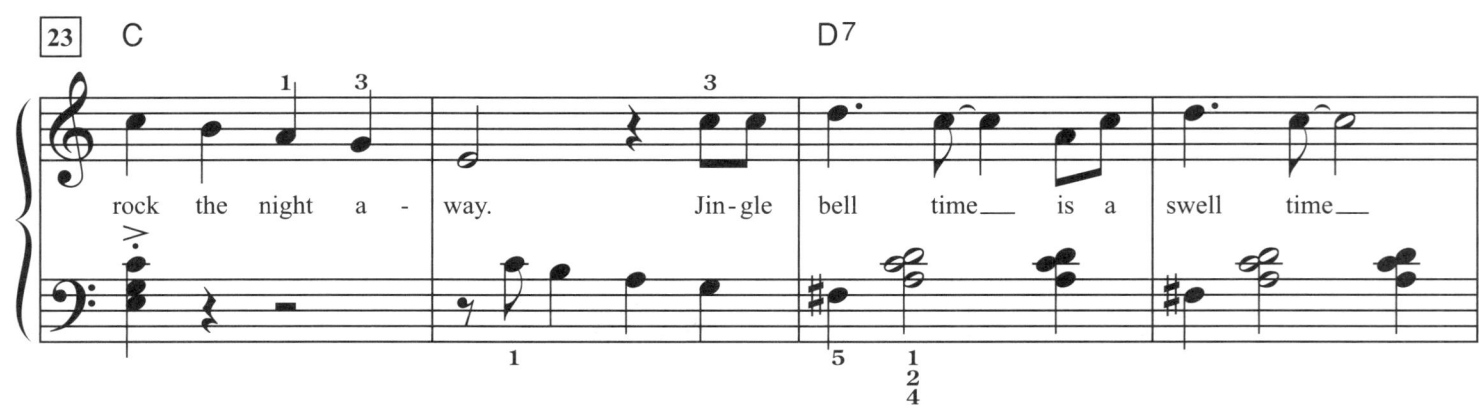

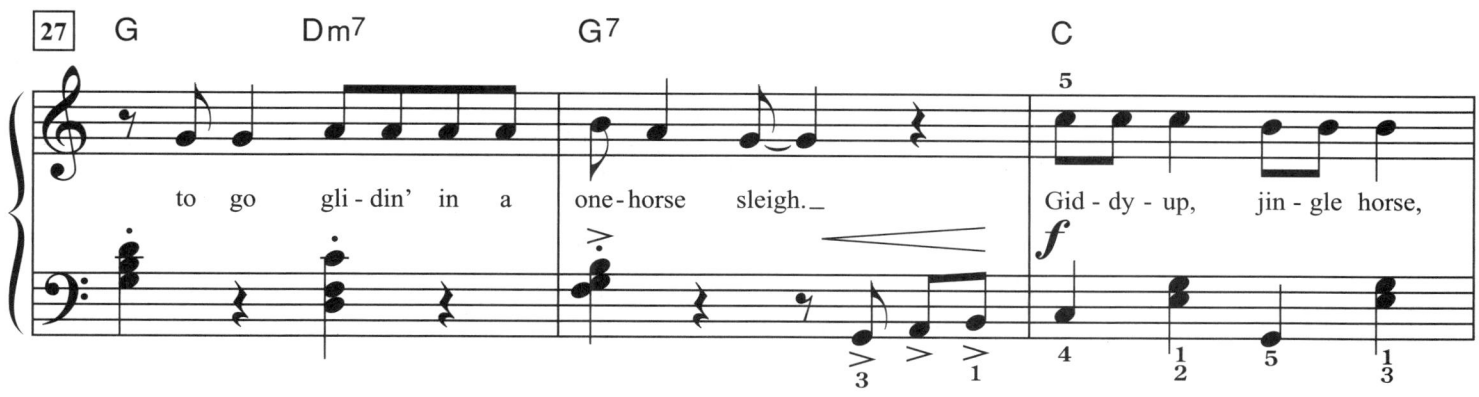
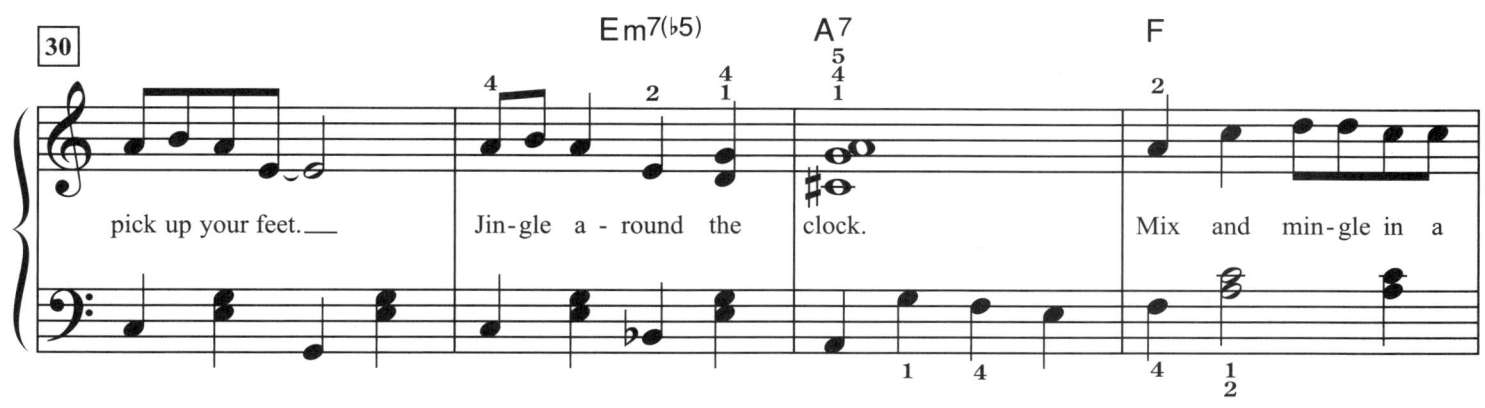
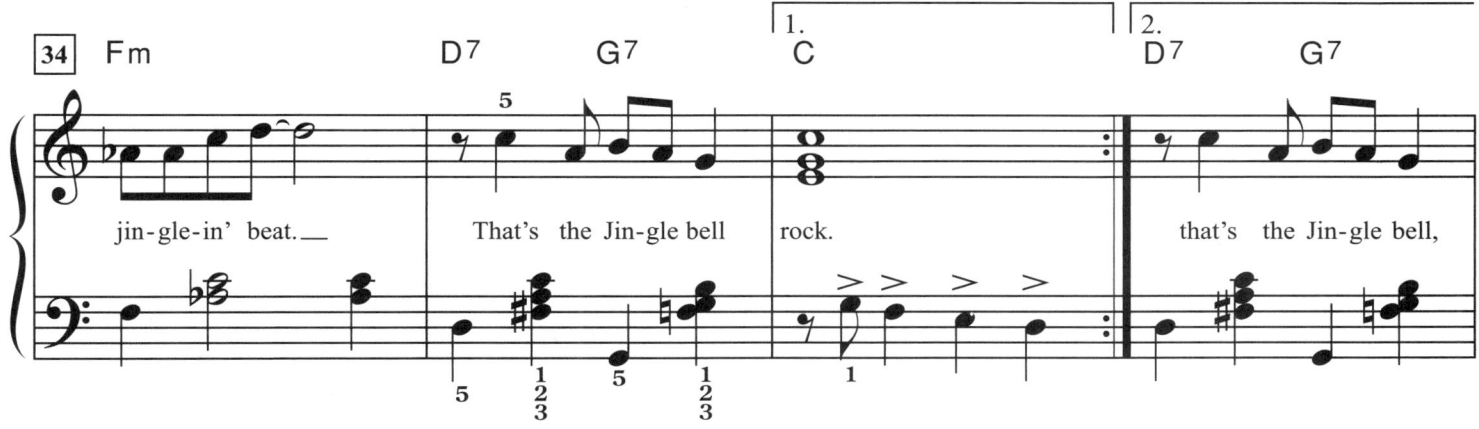
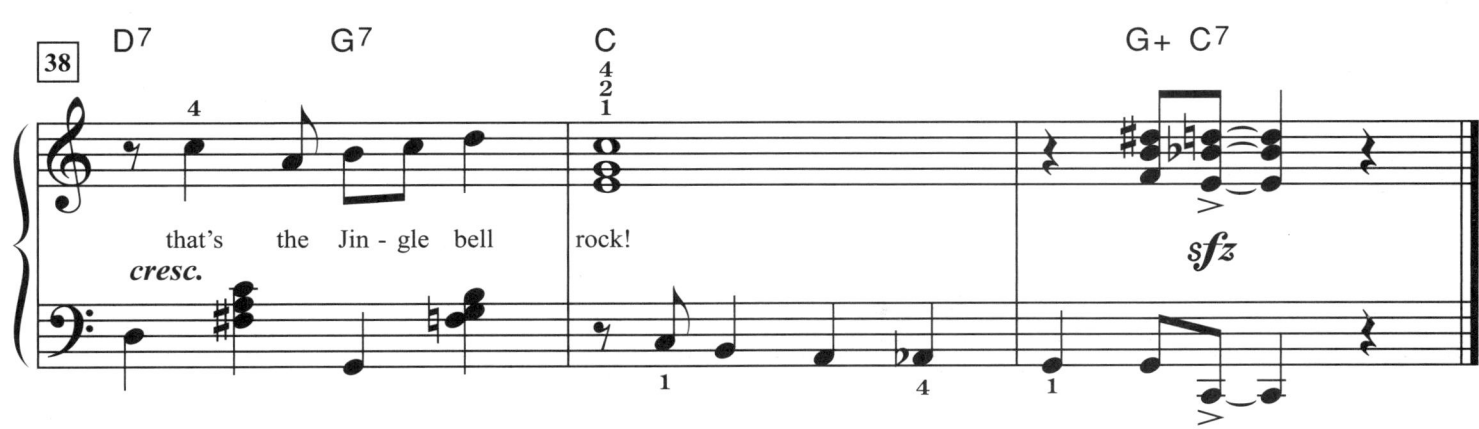